The Way of Grace: Gospel Stories for Lent

Seven Weeks of Reflection on Christ's Journey to Easter

Chuck Warnock

and

Jim Stovall

A Solid Rock Bible Series book

2025

Copyright © 2025 by Chuck Warnock and Jim Stovall

All rights reserved. This book or any portion thereof may not be reproduced or used in any manner whatsoever without the express written permission of the authors except for the use of brief quotations in a book review.

Printed in the United States of America

First Printing, 2025
ISBN 978-0-9857247-3-3

First Inning Press
Maryville, Tennessee, USA

Scripture quotations taken from The Holy Bible, New International Version® NIV®
Copyright © 1973, 1978, 1984, 2011 by Biblica, Inc.
Used with permission. All rights reserved worldwide.

Scripture quotations taken from the Revised Standard Version of the Bible, copyright © 1946, 1952, and 1971 National Council of the Churches of Christ in the United States of America. Used by permission. All rights reserved worldwide.

Cover Design: Debbie Warnock

Table of contents

WALKING TOGETHER: A LENTEN JOURNEY	**V**
THE SOLID ROCK BIBLE SERIES	IX
WHEN EVERYTHING TURNS TO DUST: AN ASH WEDNESDAY MEDITATION	**1**
WEEK 1: OUR LENTEN JOURNEY BEGINS WITH A TEST	**6**
REFLECTIONS FOR THE WEEK AHEAD	15
Tuesday Devotion: Kingdom of God	17
Thursday Devotion: The Promises of God	19
WEEK 2: WHEN WAITING MEANS WONDER	**22**
REFLECTIONS FOR THE WEEK AHEAD	28
Tuesday Devotion: Redemption and Action	29
Thursday Devotion: Pray for Peace	31
WEEK 3: FINDING GRACE IN LIFE'S HARD PLACES	**33**
REFLECTIONS FOR THE WEEK AHEAD	40
Tuesday Devotion: The Surveillance Society	41
Thursday Devotion: Rules are Rules	43
WEEK 4: THE JOURNEY HOME: A PATTERN OF DIVINE RECONCILIATION	**45**
REFLECTIONS FOR THE WEEK AHEAD	54
Tuesday Devotion: Love Your Enemies	55
Thursday Devotion: Seize the Day	57
WEEK 5: THE FRAGRANCE OF LOVE	**59**
REFLECTIONS FOR THE WEEK AHEAD	65
Tuesday Devotion: No More Excuses	66
Thursday Devotion: Where are You Planted?	68

WEEK 6: A TALE OF TWO KINGDOMS	**70**
REFLECTIONS FOR THE WEEK AHEAD	*78*
Tuesday Devotion: Fear Not Your Inadequacies	79
Thursday Devotion: Good News	81
WEEK 7: WHEN YOU ARE LOOKING FOR JESUS: A RESURRECTION STORY	**83**
REFLECTIONS FOR THE WEEK AHEAD	*90*
Tuesday Devotion: Fear and Understanding	91
Thursday Devotion: Whither Shall We Go	93
INTRODUCTION TO THE LEADER'S GUIDE	**95**
WEEK 1 LEADER'S GUIDE: OUR LENTEN JOURNEY BEGINS WITH A TEST	**98**
WEEK 2 LEADER'S GUIDE: WHEN WAITING MEANS WONDER	**102**
WEEK 3 LEADER'S GUIDE: FINDING GRACE IN LIFE'S HARD PLACES	**106**
WEEK 4 LEADER'S GUIDE: THE JOURNEY HOME	**110**
WEEK 5 LEADER'S GUIDE: THE FRAGRANCE OF LOVE	**114**
WEEK 6 LEADER'S GUIDE: A TALE OF TWO KINGDOMS	**118**
WEEK 7 LEADER'S GUIDE: WHEN YOU ARE LOOKING FOR JESUS	**122**
ACKNOWLEDGEMENTS	**127**
GRACE FOR ALL: THE PODCAST AND THE BOOK	**128**
COMING SOON: GENESIS: THE GOD WHO CALLS AND KEEPS	**130**
ABOUT THE AUTHORS	**138**

Walking Together: A Lenten Journey

An Introduction by Chuck Warnock and Jim Stovall

The season of Lent has long served as a sacred time of reflection, renewal, and spiritual deepening for Christians worldwide. This study guide emerged from a friendship that began in a high school journalism classroom and has spanned decades of shared faith, writing, and ministry. As we've walked our individual paths – one through pastoral ministry and religious writing, the other through journalism and academia – we've discovered that the greatest spiritual insights often come through joining our different perspectives in common purpose.

Our Journey Together

This study follows the rhythm of the Christian Year, specifically the lectionary readings for Year C during the season of Lent. We chose this approach because the lectionary connects us with millions of other Christians worldwide who are reading and reflecting on these same passages each week. It's a reminder that while our Lenten journey may feel personal, we're actually walking a well-worn path with fellow travelers across time and space.

Each week's study begins with Sunday's lectionary reading, but it doesn't end there. We recognize that spiritual growth happens not just in moments of corporate worship or organized study, but in the quiet spaces of our everyday lives.

That's why we've structured this guide to walk with you throughout your week.

How This Study Works

The study is organized to provide multiple points of engagement:

An Ash Wednesday meditation

Lent, of course, does not begin on a Sunday but in the middle of the week on a special day designated as Ash Wednesday. It is on that day where we begin the journey by coming face-to-face with our humanity and our relationship to God. This meditation provides a way into thinking seriously about the next 40 days.

Sunday Lessons

Each week begins with a main lesson based on the lectionary reading for that Sunday in Lent. These lessons provide historical context, theological insights, and contemporary applications of the scripture passage. They're designed to be both accessible and deep, offering something meaningful whether you're new to Bible study or have been studying scripture for years.

Daily Reflections

Following each Sunday lesson, you'll find daily reflections for Monday through Saturday. These shorter pieces help you carry the themes and insights from Sunday throughout your week, providing specific prompts for prayer, meditation, and practical application.

Mid-Week Devotionals

On Tuesdays and Thursdays, additional devotional readings offer fresh perspectives on related spiritual themes. These pieces create bridges between the main weekly lessons, helping you see new connections and layers of meaning in your Lenten journey.

An additional note: In several instances throughout this study, there are first-person references. When they appear in the Sunday lessons, they are coming from Chuck. When they are in the devotions, they are from Jim.

Leader's Guides

For each lesson, we've included detailed leader's guides that can serve multiple purposes. If you're leading a group study, these provide background material, discussion questions, and suggestions for group engagement. If you're using this book for personal study, the leader's guides offer deeper diving points for individual reflection and journal writing.

About the Authors

This project represents a unique collaboration born of an enduring friendship. We first met in high school, where we worked together on the school newspaper and yearbook staff. Those early experiences of crafting stories and meeting deadlines planted seeds that would grow in different but complementary directions.

Chuck Warnock's journey led him to pastoral ministry, serving churches across the Southeast in Georgia, North Carolina, Tennessee, and Virginia. Along the way, he maintained his connection to writing, serving as a contributing editor for various Christian publications and authoring numerous articles and a book that bridges the gap between theological insight and practical faith.

Jim Stovall pursued a path in journalism that led him through newsrooms and ultimately to the classroom, where he's shared his passion for storytelling and truth-telling with students at the University of Alabama, Emory and Henry College, and the University of Tennessee. His journey through journalism has always been informed by his faith, seeing the pursuit of truth as a sacred calling.

More biographical details can be found at the end of this volume.

Our Hope for This Study

We believe that Lent isn't just about giving something up – it's about making space for something new. Our prayer is that this study will help you create that space in your life, whether you're studying alone, with a small group, or in a larger church setting.

As you journey through these pages, you'll find that we've tried to honor both the ancient wisdom of Christian tradition and the very real challenges of living faithfully in today's world. We've drawn from our different perspectives – the journalist's eye for detail and the pastor's heart for spiritual nurture – to create a guide that we hope will help you encounter God's presence in fresh ways this Lenten season.

May this journey through Lent open new pathways of understanding, deepen your faith, and help you discover God's presence in both the wilderness and the welcome table of your life.

The Solid Rock Bible Series

This volume is the first in a set of books that we have planned titled the Solid Rock Bible Series.

These books are aimed at Sunday school classes and Bible study groups that share the authors' passion for scripture, understanding, contemplation, prayer, and devotion.

The next volume in the series will be a 12-part study of the book of Genesis, tentatively titled **Genesis: The God Who Calls and Keeps.** More information about that volume can be found at the end of this book. We expect that book to be published in the spring of 2025.

We are honored that you are reading this book, and we would love to hear from you about it. Our email addresses are Chuck (chuckwarnock@gmail.com) and Jim (jgstovall@gmail.com).

Chuck posts regularly on his website **The Rhythm of Grace,** (https://www.chuckwarnock.com) and Jim writes a monthly newsletter that can be subscribed to and found his website **JPROF.com**.

Chuck Warnock
Simpsonville, South Carolina

Jim Stovall
Maryville, Tennessee
December 2024

When Everything Turns to Dust: An Ash Wednesday Meditation

ASH Wednesday

Can you recall a time in your life when you felt rejected and abandoned? When your future seemed dark and desolate? Maybe a good thing you were counting on didn't happen. Maybe you were unable to join a group you desperately wanted to be part of. Maybe you didn't get that job that you thought would be ideal and that would assure the success of your professional career.

How did you feel?

Maybe you felt like, in modern parlance, dirt.

While such memories are painful and difficult to recall -- even if they are long past -- they are good starting point for our journey through this Lenten season.

These moments when our hopes crumble to dust offer us a visceral understanding of what we acknowledge on Ash Wednesday: our fundamental fragility.

When the priest or minister marks our foreheads with ashes and speaks those ancient words, "Remember that you are dust, and to dust you shall return," we are not just contemplating physical mortality. We recognize something we feel in our bones during those times of desolation: the impermanence of our constructions, the brittleness of our certainties, the way our carefully built plans scatter like ashes in the wind.

We have all been there. We all have those stories to tell.

But here's where the journey of Lent reveals its profound purpose: dust is not our destination, it's our starting point. Just as God once shaped humanity from the dust of the earth, breathing divine life into elemental clay, Lent offers us the opportunity to be recreated. When we submit to the mark of ashes, we're not merely acknowledging our mortality; we're offering ourselves to the Master Potter, saying, "Here I am, Lord. Reshape me. Recreate me in your image."

This reclamation and recreation project is not easy.

> *"Blessed are ye, when men shall hate you, and when they shall separate you from their company, and shall reproach you, and cast out your name as evil, for the Son of man's sake. Rejoice ye in that day, and leap for joy: for, behold, your reward is great in heaven: for in the like manner did their fathers unto the prophets."*

Like clay on the potter's wheel, we must be willing to be pressed, shaped, sometimes even broken down to be rebuilt. The disciplines of Lent -- fasting, prayer, self-examination, and acts of love -- are tools in this process of divine recreation. Each time we deny ourselves, we create space for God to work. Each prayer becomes breath that might animate new life within us. Each honest self-examination allows the Potter's hands to find another place that needs reshaping. Each act of charity helps form us more closely into the image of divine love.

Each prayer during Lent includes time for direction and re-direction.

We don't make this journey alone. Throughout these forty days, we walk with others who have chosen to acknowledge their own dusty nature and their need for divine recreation. We walk with the saints through history who have taken this path before us.

Most importantly, we walk with Christ himself, who entered fully into our dust nature, faced the ultimate abandonment on the cross, and emerged in resurrection glory.

This is the hope that guides our Lenten journey: that the God who first formed us from dust knows how to bring life from

ASH Wednesday

death, order from chaos, beauty from ashes. When we feel most acutely our dust nature -- in those moments of rejection, abandonment, and desolation-- we're actually closest to the possibility of divine recreation. For it's often only when our own constructions have crumbled that we become truly open to God's rebuilding.

This is why, at the beginning of his ministry, Jesus told all who would hear:

"Blessed are ye, when men shall hate you, and when they shall separate you from their company, and shall reproach you, and cast out your name as evil, for the Son of man's sake. Rejoice ye in that day, and leap for joy: for, behold, your reward is great in heaven: for in the like manner did their fathers unto the prophets."

The cross marked in ashes on our foreheads points us toward the journey's end: Easter morning, when Christ's resurrection will reveal the ultimate destiny of all who submit to divine recreation. Yes, we are dust, but we are dust destined for glory. Yes, the journey is difficult, but we don't walk it alone. Yes, there will be moments of desolation, but they are merely the prelude to recreation.

As we begin these forty days, let us embrace both the humility of our dust nature and the hope of divine recreation. Let us trust that the God who made us from dust the first time knows exactly how to reshape us now. Let us journey together through this sacred season, supporting each other as we submit to the Potter's hands, knowing that each step brings us closer to the risen Christ who makes all things new.

For this is the promise that burns within the ashes on our foreheads: what begins in dust and desolation can end in resurrection and glory. The journey will not be easy, but it leads us home, to the very heart of God, who creates, recreates, and ultimately resurrects.

Week 1: Our Lenten Journey Begins with a Test

Week 1: Beginning With a Test

The season of Lent stretches before us – forty days, not counting Sundays, leading us toward the profound events of Holy Week. Just as Jesus spent forty days in the wilderness being tested before beginning his ministry, we now embark on our own journey of spiritual preparation. And fittingly, our path begins where his did – with a test.

Luke 4:1-13 NIV

Jesus, full of the Holy Spirit, left the Jordan and was led by the Spirit into the wilderness, ² where for forty days he was tempted by the devil. He ate nothing during those days, and at the end of them he was hungry.

³ The devil said to him, "If you are the Son of God, tell this stone to become bread."

⁴ Jesus answered, "It is written: 'Man shall not live on bread alone.'"

⁵ The devil led him up to a high place and showed him in an instant all the kingdoms of the world. ⁶ And he said to him, "I will give you all their authority and splendor; it has been given to me, and I can give it to anyone I want to. ⁷ If you worship me, it will all be yours."

⁸ Jesus answered, "It is written: 'Worship the Lord your God and serve him only.'"

⁹ The devil led him to Jerusalem and had him stand on the highest point of the temple. "If you are the Son of God," he said, "throw yourself down from here.

¹⁰ For it is written:

"'He will command his angels concerning you to guard you carefully;

*11 they will lift you up in their hands,
so that you will not strike your foot against a stone.]"*

12 Jesus answered, "It is said: 'Do not put the Lord your God to the test.'"

13 When the devil had finished all this tempting, he left him until an opportune time.

When Temptation is Really a Test

Testing. That word alone can stir anxiety in many of us. I vividly remember sitting in my college dorm room the night before my first Western Civilization test, realizing with growing dread that I didn't know the material. This was long before the days of online study groups and internet resources – you were pretty much on your own. While I managed to pass that test, I certainly didn't distinguish myself. My moment of freshman panic that night taught me the importance of preparing for a test. It's a lesson I've never forgotten.

But testing in Scripture carries a different weight and a different purpose. When God sends a test – which is often called "temptations" in the Bible - it isn't to catch us unprepared or see us fail. Instead, it offers an opportunity for us to prove ourselves faithful, to demonstrate trust, to grow stronger. Think of Abraham, receiving God's remarkable promise of family and land. The test came immediately – would he trust enough to leave everything familiar behind? Immediately Abraham packed up his family and possessions and set out, following God's lead into the unknown. Yes, Abraham stumbled in other tests along the way, but in this crucial moment of challenge, he succeeded.

Week 1: Beginning With a Test

Or consider Moses, called by God to lead Israel out of Egyptian bondage. Despite his stuttering speech and lack of confidence, Moses stepped into his calling. Through his willingness to obey despite his limitations, Moses passed the test of faithfulness that transformed both him and a nation.

These biblical tests were opportunities for faithfulness. Many succeeded – though some failed, too. King David, a man after God's own heart, provides one of Scripture's most sobering examples of failing when tested by temptation. Yet even these failures serve to teach us about God's mercy and our need for something more than our own strength.

This brings us to Jesus's testing – usually called his temptation – in the wilderness. His experience provides crucial insights for our own Lenten journey. We know, of course, that Jesus passed every test flawlessly, and we'll explore the deep significance of that success.

The Obvious Thing about These Tests

My wife and I had the same Old Testament professor in college, though at different times. I found him rather boring, while Debbie thought he was brilliant. But one phrase he used stuck with both of us. Whenever we encountered testing or temptation in Scripture, he would remind us of temptation's three fundamental categories: the lust of the flesh, the lust of the eyes, and the pride of life.

This framework comes directly from 1 John 2:15-17:

"Do not love the world or anything in the world... For everything in the world—the lust of the flesh, the lust of the eyes, and the pride of life—comes not from the Father, but from the world."

These three categories represent our core vulnerabilities to temptation. As human beings, we're susceptible to the following:

things that give us pleasure: food, fun, excitement, romance, and so on – that's the lust of the flesh;

things that are attractive in our sight, like when David saw Bathsheba bathing on the rooftop; and,

things that feed our egos like compliments or power – that's the pride of life.

These categories of desire and their consequences appear throughout human experience, from the Garden of Eden to our own daily struggles.

So, of course, if we have God incarnate in the person of Jesus, Satan attacked what he thought would be the human weaknesses of Jesus:

For appetite, bread to satisfy his hunger after forty days of fasting.

For ambition, the kingdoms of the world visible in all their dazzling glory.

For arrogance, the chance to command angels in a spectacular display of supernatural power.

Rather than analyze each temptation individually, let's draw out three practical lessons that can guide our own spiritual journey.

Lesson Number One:

There Are No Shortcuts to Doing the Father's Will

Every temptation Satan offered Jesus represented a shortcut. Consider the bread – after forty days of fasting, Jesus was genuinely hungry. The round stones on the ground before him even resembled freshly baked loaves of bread. Why not just end the fast now? He'd made it forty days already! But Jesus resisted, quoting Scripture in response. This wasn't a spur-of-

Week 1: Beginning With a Test

the-moment reaction; it reflected deep preparation and conviction. Jesus knew this marked the beginning of his journey of obedience, and he wouldn't compromise now.

When the appeal to Jesus' hunger failed, Satan showed Jesus all the world's kingdoms, claiming authority to give them away. All of the kingdoms of the world could be his now, Satan told Jesus, if Jesus would just bow down and worship him.

Was Satan telling the truth about his power over the world's kingdoms? Many commentators debate this point. But Jesus didn't engage in that debate – you don't argue with the Father of Lies because lies are his native language. Jesus knew that one day, every kingdom would indeed recognize him as King of Kings and Lord of Lords. That authority, however, would come through obedience to the Father, not through shortcuts.

Finally, Satan took Jesus to the Temple's highest point, suggesting a dramatic display of divine power. Imagine the scene – angels swooping in to rescue the Messiah as crowds watched in amazement. Instant followers, instant acclaim! But Jesus knew that true ministry required something different: three years of teaching, countless hours healing the sick, feeding the hungry, befriending outcasts, and ultimately facing rejection, crucifixion, and death. No shortcuts would fulfill the Father's will.

**Lesson Number Two:
The End Does Not Justify the Means**

Since shortcuts didn't appeal to Jesus, Satan tried another approach. Satan's basic pitch was expediency: You can have it all right now. It's going to be yours anyway – why not speed up the process? Play by the world's rules just this once!

We face similar temptations today. I've heard of churches generating attendance spikes by offering visitors chances to win cars, furniture, money – even assault rifles! – to attract people to Sunday services. The justification always sounds the same: "If we can get just one person to hear the gospel, it's worth it." But this reasoning fundamentally misunderstands God's methods. The end never justifies unethical means.

Yes, Satan was right that Jesus would eventually receive all authority. But compromising God's principles to achieve God's purposes is still compromise. There is only one way to do God's will – the right way.

Lesson Number Three:
The Past Does Not Predict the Future

Now that we have looked at what the temptations had in common, let's look at the important accomplishment of Jesus in the desert, which brings us to the number forty. The number forty usually concerns time in Scripture, indicating a sufficient amount of time to bring a task or situation to completion. For example in Genesis 7, the account of the flood, God sent rain for forty days, enough to flood Noah's world. In Exodus 24, Moses spends forty days on Mount Sinai receiving the law from God. And, of course, after spending three days in the belly of great sea creature, the reluctant prophet Jonah preached repentance to Nineveh for forty days. All of these examples, and others, illustrate a sufficient amount of time for God's purposes to be realized.

However, the most significant parallel to Jesus's forty days in the wilderness comes from Israel's forty years in the desert. After Israel failed to trust God and enter the Promised Land, that faithless generation was condemned to wander forty years in wilderness testing.

In the 40-days of temptation, Jesus accomplished what God's people had failed to achieve before – faithfulness to God. Where Israel had doubted and faltered, Jesus trusted and obeyed. Where Israel feared God wouldn't provide, Jesus knew the Father's care was certain.

Week 1: Beginning With a Test

This faithfulness of Jesus matters profoundly to us. Jesus becomes our example and resource. We don't have to be perfect because he was perfect for us. We can face our own tests not through personal strength, but through his proven faithfulness.

As we begin our Lenten journey, we carry these twin truths: we know resurrection awaits at the journey's end, and we know that where we have failed, Jesus succeeded. Hold both close to your heart as we journey with him toward Easter.

Closing Prayer:

Loving God, as we journey through this wilderness of Lent, grant us the courage to face our temptations honestly and the strength to choose faithfully. Help us recognize the angels you send to minister to us and make us ministers of your grace to others. Guide us through these forty days of reflection and renewal, that we might emerge more deeply rooted in your love. Amen.

Reflections for the week ahead

In this section, we have a combination of questions for reflection and devotional readings that provide personal insights designed to help you on your Lenten journey. The devotional readings are taken from the ***Grace for All*** podcast, a daily devotional podcast produced by the congregation of First United Methodist Church in Maryville, Tennessee.

We highly recommend listening and subscribing to this five-minute daily podcast. It can be found on the [church website](https://1stchurch.org/extras/podcast) (https://1stchurch.org/extras/podcast) or on Apple Podcasts, Spotify, or anywhere you get your podcasts.

Monday: Consider what "wilderness" means in your life. What barren places or challenging situations are you facing? How might your current challenges be preparing you for what lies ahead?

Tuesday: Read the devotion **"Kingdom of God"** on the following pages. How did Christ's time in the wilderness prepare him to make the idea of the Kingdom of God, a central idea of his ministry? Jesus reduces the Ten Commands down to two. Is it really that simple?

Wednesday: Reflect on the second temptation of Jesus – the offer of worldly power and glory. Where are you tempted to choose power over purpose? How might you redefine success in terms of service rather than control?

Thursday: Read the devotion **"The Promises of God"** on the following pages. This is an Old Testament story. What relevance does it have for us in this season of Lent?

Friday: Jesus chose God's way over the easy way. Identify one situation in your life where you're tempted to take shortcuts or

Week 1: Beginning With a Test

compromise your values for quick results. How might choosing the harder, more faithful path lead to deeper growth?

Saturday: After Jesus' temptation, angels came to minister to him. Look back over your own times of testing. Who or what has God sent to support and strengthen you? Today, be mindful of how you might be called to be that support for someone else in their wilderness.

Tuesday Devotion: Kingdom of God

Mark 12:28-34 NIV

28 One of the teachers of the law came and heard them debating. Noticing that Jesus had given them a good answer, he asked him, "Of all the commandments, which is the most important?"

29 "The most important one," answered Jesus, "is this: 'Hear, O Israel: The Lord our God, the Lord is one. 30 Love the Lord your God with all your heart and with all your soul and with all your mind and with all your strength.' 31 The second is this: 'Love your neighbor as yourself.' There is no commandment greater than these."

32 "Well said, teacher," the man replied. "You are right in saying that God is one and there is no other but him. 33 To love him with all your heart, with all your understanding and with all your strength, and to love your neighbor as yourself is more important than all burnt offerings and sacrifices."

34 When Jesus saw that he had answered wisely, he said to him, "You are not far from the kingdom of God." And from then on no one dared ask him any more questions.

When we recite the apostles creed, we usually say the lines "*born of the Virgin Mary*" and "*suffered under Pontius Pilate*" with nothing in between. In doing that we skip over the time that Jesus spent on earth and his ministry to those who are fortunate enough to hear him in person.

During his time on earth, Jesus declared the establishment of the Kingdom of God. He repeated this phrase again and again, and he often began parables with *"The Kingdom of God is like..."* What Jesus was saying was that there was a new way of thinking about God and a new hope for all of humankind. The Kingdom of God was at hand, and Jesus was inviting us to be a part of it.

His words to the scribe in this story are important. The scribe shows a depth of understanding of what Jesus was saying that was unusual for his day. It was obvious from the scribe's words that he had discovered something new and unique about Jesus. Jesus compliments him by saying that he is "not far" from the kingdom.

The question for us then is how far are we from the central message of Jesus's ministry?

Grace for All podcast, episode 2

https://graceforall.captivate.fm/episode/the-kingdom-of-god

Thursday Devotion: The Promises of God

Joshua 1:1–2, 5–6 NIV

After the death of Moses the servant of the Lord, the Lord said to Joshua son of Nun, Moses' aide: ² "Moses my servant is dead. Now then, you and all these people, get ready to cross the Jordan River into the land I am about to give to them—to the Israelites.

⁵ No one will be able to stand against you all the days of your life. As I was with Moses, so I will be with you; I will never leave you nor forsake you. ⁶ Be strong and courageous, because you will lead these people to inherit the land I swore to their ancestors to give them.

In this passage, we see the transfer of leadership of the children of Israel from Moses to Joshua. It is a political transfer, but God infuses it with his presence and makes it holy. God makes some incredible promises to Joshua. No one, he tells Joshua, will be able to stand before him throughout his life. He promises Joshua success.

Joshua, of course, has his role to play. He has his decisions to make. He is not some wind-up toy that God simply sets in motion. He is a human being with free will to make his own choices, but God cautioned him to follow in the ways of Moses, and to turn neither to the left or to the right. Joshua will be successful only as long as he acts in concert with God.

This is a powerful passage, one that demonstrates God's direct intervention into the life of a person. Joshua is to "go and do," as we all are, but we are always to go with the Lord. What do we see and hear when we imagine the conversation between God and Joshua? Does God treat us any differently from Joshua?

Week 1: Beginning With a Test

God makes promises to us. What are we to do to fulfill our part of those promises? Joshua, as we know from later parts of the story, had many successes in leading his people into the land of Canaan. What successes does God have in store for us?

Let us pray together: Dear God, give us the strength to fulfill your promises. Give us the wisdom to turn, neither to the right, nor to the left, but to follow in your paths, and to act with your guidance. Amen.

Grace for All podcast, episode 4

https://graceforall.captivate.fm/episode/the-promises-of-god

Notes

Week 2: When Waiting Means Wonder

Luke 9:28-36 NRSV

²⁸ Now about eight days after these sayings Jesus took with him Peter and John and James and went up on the mountain to pray. ²⁹ And while he was praying, the appearance of his face changed, and his clothes became dazzling white.

³⁰ Suddenly they saw two men, Moses and Elijah, talking to him. ³¹ They appeared in glory and were speaking of his departure, which he was about to accomplish at Jerusalem.

³² Now Peter and his companions were weighed down with sleep; but since they had stayed awake, they saw his glory and the two men who stood with him.

³³ Just as they were leaving him, Peter said to Jesus, "Master, it is good for us to be here; let us make three dwellings, one for you, one for Moses, and one for Elijah"—not knowing what he said.

³⁴ While he was saying this, a cloud came and overshadowed them; and they were terrified as they entered the cloud. ³⁵ Then from the cloud came a voice that said, "This is my Son, my Chosen; listen to him!" 36 When the voice had spoken, Jesus was found alone. And they kept silent, and in those days told no one any of the things they had seen.

Week 2: When Waiting Means Wonder

From the Desert to the Mountain, Our Journey Continues

From the solitude of Jesus' temptation in the desert to the mountain of transfiguration, our Lenten journey takes us literally to new heights, both physically and spiritually. Jesus and three of his most trusted disciples, Peter, James and John, will have an experience unlike any other. Amazingly, the disciples could have missed it, but fortunately for them and us, they stayed alert. Staying patiently alert isn't always easy. Believe me, I know, and I'm a pastor.

The Reward of Patient Watching

As a pastor, I carried an inner secret: I never liked Easter sunrise services. It wasn't just because Easter Sunday was already the church's busiest day of the year. The real reason was that I had never experienced a sunrise service in a setting that truly captured the glory we were celebrating – the resurrection of Christ.

My first attempt at leading one in our small Virginia town was well-intended but disappointing. Early one cold Easter Sunday morning, our small group gathered under a picnic shelter in the town park. Just as we reached our final hymn, "Up From the Grave He Arose," we should have seen the sunrise.

Unfortunately, the actual sunrise was completely blocked by the shelter's roof and a nearby building. An Easter sunrise service without the sunrise feels incomplete.

But the next year, everything changed. A neighboring Methodist church invited us to join them for a community service on their member's horse farm – specifically, on top of a small mountain. Though it meant rising even earlier and traveling further in the cold darkness, something told me to stay alert for what might unfold.

What I didn't know was that the mountain faced east over a sprawling valley. As we sang our Easter hymns in the pre-dawn chill, the sky before us slowly transformed – first with a warm orange glow, then bursting into full glory as the sun emerged. At that precise moment, horses in the valley below began to gallop, as if they too were celebrating the risen Christ.

Standing there with tears in my eyes, I realized that sometimes the most glorious moments come to those who wait expectantly in the darkness. After that morning, I had a new reverence for Easter sunrise services.

This experience of waiting in darkness for a glimpse of glory reminds me of another group of people who found themselves struggling to stay awake one night on a mountainside, not knowing they were about to witness something extraordinary.

The Journey to the Mountain

By this point in Luke's Gospel, Jesus' ministry was in full swing. He had performed countless miracles: healing the sick, casting out impure spirits, feeding thousands, calming storms, and even raising the dead. Then came Peter's pivotal declaration: "You are God's Messiah." It was a moment of clarity, followed by Jesus' sobering words about his coming death.

Eight days after this conversation, Jesus chose his inner circle—Peter, James, and John—to accompany him up the mountain to pray. What followed would become one of the most extraordinary moments in their journey with Christ.

The Weight of Weariness

Luke tells us the disciples were "weighed down with sleep"—a phrase that captures perfectly that heavy, consuming exhaustion we know so well. Yet somehow, through what must have been tremendous effort, they managed to stay awake. Because they remained alert, they witnessed something extraordinary.

Week 2: When Waiting Means Wonder

Imagine if they had succumbed to sleep! They would have missed seeing Jesus transformed before their eyes, his face altered and his clothes dazzling white. They would have missed the appearance of Moses—the great lawgiver who led Israel from bondage to freedom—and Elijah—the mighty prophet who stood against false gods and witnessed God's power in spectacular ways.

Both these men had extraordinary departures from this world: Moses, buried by God Himself in an unknown grave, and Elijah, taken to heaven in a chariot of fire. Now here they were, speaking with Jesus about his own approaching "departure" in Jerusalem.

Staying Alert to God's Presence

The disciples' experience holds profound meaning for us today. While we may not witness a physical transfiguration, we too can miss glimpses of God's glory when we become spiritually drowsy. Our modern lives are filled with distractions that can weigh us down just as heavily as physical exhaustion weighed on the disciples.

Peter's reaction to this magnificent sight is telling. He suggests building dwellings for Jesus, Moses, and Elijah—perhaps trying to capture and contain this holy moment. Luke tells us Peter "did not know what he said." Peter sounds very human – missing the point because he was trying to manage what God was doing.

The Call to Holy Anticipation

God's voice from the cloud cut through Peter's confusion with crystal clarity: "This is my Son, my Chosen; listen to him!" This command rings true for us today. Spiritual alertness isn't about building structures or creating programs—it's about staying awake to God's presence and listening to Jesus.

The story's aftermath is equally instructive. When they came down from the mountain, they encountered a father whose son needed healing—a healing the disciples had been unable to perform. Even after witnessing such glory, they still struggled with doubt and fear that limited their spiritual effectiveness.

Living in Expectant Hope

What weighs us down today? Perhaps it's anxiety about the future, the pace of modern life, or simple physical weariness. Maybe it's doubt, fear, or the countless distractions that pull us away from God's presence. Yet like the disciples, if we stay spiritually alert—even when we feel weighed down—we position ourselves to witness God's glory in our midst.

This isn't about straining to stay physically awake during prayer -- though that can be important. It's about maintaining an awareness of God's presence and activity in our lives. It's about being ready to recognize the holy moments that break into our ordinary days, just as that Easter sunrise broke through the darkness, revealing unexpected glory.

Prayer

Lord, when we are weighed down by life's demands and distractions, help us stay alert to Your presence. Give us the strength to remain spiritually awake, that we might glimpse Your glory in our daily lives. Amen.

Week 2: When Waiting Means Wonder

Reflections for the week ahead

In this section, we have a combination of questions for reflection and devotional readings that provide personal insights designed to help you on your Lenten journey. The devotional readings are taken from the **Grace for All** podcast, a daily devotional podcast produced by the congregation of First United Methodist Church in Maryville, Tennessee.

We highly recommend listening and subscribing to this five-minute daily podcast. It can be found on the church website (https://1stchurch.org/extras/podcast) or on Apple Podcasts, Spotify, or anywhere you get your podcasts.

Monday: Consider a time when waiting led to wonder in your own life. What helped you stay alert to God's presence?

Tuesday: Read the devotion **"Redemption and Action"** on the following pages. Peter is redeemed, but there is something else that Jesus then demands. How do you feel about "Feed my sheep"?

Wednesday: Find a quiet place to watch a sunrise or sunset today. Use this time to practice spiritual alertness and meditation.

Thursday: Read the devotion **"Pray for Peace."** Is that your daily prayer? Have you heard God's response?

Friday: Practice listening prayer today, following God's command to "listen to him!" What do you hear in the silence?

Saturday: Look for unexpected glimpses of God's glory in ordinary moments today, just as the disciples saw Jesus transfigured in an ordinary night of prayer.

Tuesday Devotion: Redemption and Action

John 21:15-17 NIV

> [15] When they had finished eating, Jesus said to Simon Peter, "Simon son of John, do you love me more than these?" "Yes, Lord," he said, "you know that I love you." Jesus said, "Feed my lambs."
>
> [16] Again Jesus said, "Simon son of John, do you love me?" He answered, "Yes, Lord, you know that I love you." Jesus said, "Take care of my sheep."
>
> [17] The third time he said to him, "Simon son of John, do you love me?" Peter was hurt because Jesus asked him the third time, "Do you love me?" He said, "Lord, you know all things; you know that I love you." Jesus said, "Feed my sheep.

At one point during his ministry on earth, Jesus called Peter "a rock" and said that Peter would be the foundation of his church. Not long after that, Peter was put to the test, and he failed spectacularly. When Jesus was arrested and tried, Peter denied Jesus three times.

What happened to that man who was supposed to be the Rock, who was supposed to be the foundation of the new religion and the new life that Christ taught?

In this passage, we see Christ, going to some length to redeem Peter. Yes, Peter denied Christ. It was no accident. He had done it three times. So here, Jesus asks Peter three times, "Do you love me?" Of course he does, Peter says, why do you keep asking?

This scene tells us something about our own lives and our relationship to Christ. We failed spectacularly, not just once but many times. We do the wrong thing. We say the wrong thing. We let our cowardice overcome our courage.

Week 2: When Waiting Means Wonder

And yet, for every time we fail, Christ offers us a way back. Do you love me? That's the question he continues to ask. Of course, we do. Then feed my sheep, he says. Do not just confess yourself, but put your confession into action. Feed my sheep.

Grace for All podcast, episode 6

https://graceforall.captivate.fm/episode/redemption-and-action

Thursday Devotion: Pray for Peace

John 14:27 NIV

> *Peace I leave with you; my peace I give you. I do not give to you as the world gives. Do not let your hearts be troubled and do not be afraid.*

Most of us pray for peace at some point in our lives. The prayer for "peace on earth" is one that we echo from what the angels sang at the birth of Christ. We wish the tribes and nations, including our own, would be more peaceful. We wish that armies would stop fighting each other.

In our political and social lives, most of us crave peace. We wish to see an end to the bickering, the backbiting, the fighting, and the constant divisions with which the news media bombards us every day.

In our personal lives, we wish that family members, again, including ourselves, could just learn to get along. Family gatherings of any type should be a time of peace. All too often they are a time of conflict.

Jesus, in this verse, has promised his peace, and we want to cash in on that promise. We are likely to skip over the part where he says "my peace" is what he is giving us. We tend not to think very deeply about the words "I do not give to you as the world gives."

So what is it that Jesus is offering us? It certainly is not the peace of our definition, the "peace on earth" that we so desperately seek at all levels. The peace of Jesus is something different, something else, something very special. It is the peace of the Kingdom of Heaven, which Christ came to declare in his ministry on earth. It is the peace of knowing that whatever wars and conflicts are occurring around us, we can

Week 2: When Waiting Means Wonder

have the peace of Jesus with us to calm the storms, not on the outside of our lives but those storms that are in our hearts.

Grace for All podcast, episode 9

https://graceforall.captivate.fm/episode/pray-for-peace

Week 3: Finding Grace in Life's Hard Places

Week 3: Finding Grace in Life's Hard Places

Luke 13:1-9 NIV

Now there were some present at that time who told Jesus about the Galileans whose blood Pilate had mixed with their sacrifices. [2] Jesus answered, "Do you think that these Galileans were worse sinners than all the other Galileans because they suffered this way? [3] I tell you, no! But unless you repent, you too will all perish. [4] Or those eighteen who died when the tower in Siloam fell on them—do you think they were more guilty than all the others living in Jerusalem? [5] I tell you, no! But unless you repent, you too will all perish."

[6] Then he told this parable: "A man had a fig tree growing in his vineyard, and he went to look for fruit on it but did not find any. [7] So he said to the man who took care of the vineyard, 'For three years now I've been coming to look for fruit on this fig tree and haven't found any. Cut it down! Why should it use up the soil?'

[8] "'Sir,' the man replied, 'leave it alone for one more year, and I'll dig around it and fertilize it. [9] If it bears fruit next year, fine! If not, then cut it down.'"

Surprised by Grace

Today's scripture is a difficult story containing two accounts of massive loss of life and its attendant suffering. As we reach the midpoint of our Lenten journey, honest reflection on this passage can lead us to some uncomfortable truths.

One of humanity's unattractive traits is our quickness to judge others' misfortunes. We often blame the victims of tragedy rather than simply empathizing with their plight. And sometimes, we even imply that we could have handled a situation better than those who suffered through it. This week's Gospel reading challenges these deep-seated human tendencies, inviting us instead into a frank encounter with divine grace.

This tension between judgment and grace is powerfully illustrated by an extraordinary event that took place in Scotland just after World War II. In 1945, a young German soldier sat in a prisoner of war camp, wrestling with the weight of his homeland's failures and his own broken dreams. Jürgen Moltmann had entered the war filled with the hollow arrogance of Nazi ideology. Now captured and imprisoned on foreign soil, Moltmann was confronted with photographic evidence of the horrors of the Third Reich's genocide. But despite his profound despair and overwhelming guilt, Moltmann encountered the unexpected: *grace.*

The Scottish Christians working with the German prisoners didn't judge them or preach cheap platitudes. Instead, they extended simple kindness, treating their former enemies with dignity and compassion. They shared their Bibles, their time, and most importantly, their genuine concern for the young POWs. Through their actions, Moltmann encountered what he would later describe as "the divine presence in suffering."

This experience transformed him from a despairing prisoner into one of the twentieth century's most influential Christian

Week 3: Finding Grace in Life's Hard Places

scholars – the theologian of hope. Moltmann wrote that we find God not in power or triumph, but in suffering and vulnerability.

When Tragedy Demands Answers

As in Moltmann's time, first-century Judean culture struggled to make sense of suffering and tragedy. In our passage, a group of breathless messengers is quick to tell Jesus about a horrible incident -- Galilean pilgrims to the Temple, along with their animals destined for sacrifice, were slaughtered together by Pilate's soldiers. These distraught bearers-of-bad-news seem to think that those killed must have done something bad to deserve their fate.

It's a deeply human response. As Rabbi Harold Kushner notes in his profound book, *When Bad Things Happen to Good People*, we want to believe in a world where good things happen to good people and vice-versa. It helps us feel that the universe is fair, that we get what we deserve.

Instead, Jesus challenges this simplistic understanding.

"Do you think that these Galileans were worse sinners than all the other Galileans because they suffered this way?" he asks. *"I tell you, no!"*

Then Jesus mentions another tragedy, this time an accident. Eighteen people had been killed when the Tower of Siloam collapsed. Again, Jesus asks the same penetrating question,

"Were they more guilty than others...?"

Like Moltmann discovered centuries later in that Scottish POW camp, your suffering is not the wrath of God poured out on you for your own sins. Suffering can be caused by others, like Pontius Pilate and his Roman centurions. Or suffering may be the result of an accident, like a failed building. Rather than trite explanations or victim blaming, Jesus points us toward a more fitting approach -- finding God's presence in suffering.

> **In Jesus' telling, the fig tree symbolized Israel. For centuries, they had failed to produce the fruit of faithfulness. Yet, Jesus offers hope and another chance for God's people to blossom and bloom, again.**

Grace Before We Know It

This is where Jesus begins to reshape our understanding about tragedy, judgment, and grace. God is at work, even when we do not know it. Centuries later, John Wesley would call this God's prevenient grace. Jesus points to that deeper truth through the parable of the fig tree.

"A man had a fig tree growing in his vineyard," Jesus tells them, *"and he went to look for fruit on it but did not find any."*

The owner wanted to cut it down, and that response seems reasonable for an unproductive tree. After all, three years was the expected growing cycle. The tree should be cut it down to make room for one that will bear fruit. But the gardener intervenes, proposing another year of careful cultivation:

"Sir, leave it alone for one more year, and I'll dig around it and fertilize it."

Of course, in Jesus' telling, the fig tree symbolized Israel. For centuries, they had failed to produce the fruit of faithfulness. Yet, Jesus offers hope and another chance for God's people to blossom and bloom, again.

In this simple story, we see a profound truth about God's patient work in our lives. Like the gardener tending the unfruitful tree, God's grace is already at work before we recognize it. Just as Moltmann encountered God's love through unexpected kindness before he understood it, the divine gardener cultivates our growth even when we show no signs of fruit.

Beyond Judgment to Hope

This challenges our natural inclination to judge others and ourselves. When tragedy strikes, we often ask the wrong questions: "Why did this happen?" or "Who's to blame?" Instead, we might ask, as Moltmann and Kushner both suggest, "Where is God present here and now?"

Wisely, the gardener in Jesus's parable doesn't speculate about why the tree is barren or assign blame. Instead, he focuses on creating conditions for growth. This is prevenient grace in action - patient, persistent, and promising. It's the same grace those Scottish Christians showed to their former enemies. It's the same grace that transforms judgment into hope.

Living in Grace

Like those who brought tragic news to Jesus, we often want simple answers to life's complex sorrows. However, Jesus points us toward a different way. We can't always explain tragedy, but we can respond to it with grace.

The Christians who helped Moltmann didn't know their kindness would transform a despairing soldier into a beacon of theological hope. The gardener couldn't guarantee the fig tree would bear fruit. But both demonstrated the patient work of grace. Both created space for God's love to take root and grow out of a tragic situation.

In this Lenten season, as we pause midway in our journey, we're called to do the same. Rather than demand instant fruit, we can learn from the Divine Gardener, and patiently cultivate growth. We can suspend judgment, look for God's presence in difficult places, and extend to others the same patient tending we've received. When we do that, we will discover with

Moltmann and countless others, hope grows best in the soil of grace.

Prayer: Patient Gardener, help us recognize your nurturing presence in our lives, especially in times of difficulty. Give us grace to extend to others the same patience you show to us. Transform our judgment into hope, our condemnation into love. Amen.

Week 3: Finding Grace in Life's Hard Places

Reflections for the week ahead

In this section, we have a combination of questions for reflection and devotional readings that provide personal insights designed to help you on your Lenten journey. The devotional readings are taken from the ***Grace for All*** podcast, a daily devotional podcast produced by the congregation of First United Methodist Church in Maryville, Tennessee.

We highly recommend listening and subscribing to this five-minute daily podcast. It can be found on the [church website (https://1stchurch.org/extras/podcast)](https://1stchurch.org/extras/podcast) or on Apple Podcasts, Spotify, or anywhere you get your podcasts.

Monday: Notice where God's grace might be quietly at work in your life, even in difficult circumstances.

Tuesday: Read the devotion **"The Surveillance Society"** on the following pages. God promises to watch over us in the most difficult time, "even though we walk through the darkest valley." How real is that promise in your life?

Wednesday: Reflect on times when others showed you unexpected grace. How did that grace change you?

Thursday: Read the devotion **"Rules are Rules"** on the following pages. Has following the rules ever led you or someone you know astray or kept them from doing the right thing?

Friday: Look for opportunities to extend grace to others, especially those you might be tempted to judge.

Saturday: Meditate on how experiencing God's patience changes how you view others' struggles.

Tuesday Devotion: The Surveillance Society

Psalm 23 NIV

The LORD is my shepherd, I lack nothing. He makes me lie down in green pastures,

he leads me beside quiet waters, he refreshes my soul.

He guides me along the right paths for his name's sake.

Even though I walk through the darkest valley,

I will fear no evil, for you are with me;

your rod and your staff, they comfort me.

You prepare a table before me in the presence of my enemies.

You anoint my head with oil; my cup overflows.

Surely your goodness and love will follow me all the days of my life, and I will dwell in the house of the LORD forever.

When my grandson was born, in one of the many conversations I had with my son (his father), we talked about where the baby would sleep and what kind of a setup the parents had for him in their house. The parents wanted the baby to sleep in a separate room, but they were putting a video camera there so they could keep watch over him. My son mentioned that the child would inevitably grow up in a "surveillance society."

I think about that occasionally when I hear Biblical phrases such as the one in this famous Psalm about the Lord being a shepherd who watches over his sleep.

If we are trying to live within the Kingdom of God, we too are living in a "surveillance society" – one that is watched over by God, who doesn't need a video camera. He is always there with

Week 3: Finding Grace in Life's Hard Places

us. No matter where I am, God is there. It is one of his consistent promises throughout all of scripture. Just as the parents provide and care for a new infant, the Lord is indeed our all-seeing shepherd, and we shall not want for whatever we truly need.

Grace for All podcast, episode 13

https://graceforall.captivate.fm/episode/the-surveillance-society

Thursday Devotion: Rules are Rules

Luke 13:10-17 NIV

On a Sabbath Jesus was teaching in one of the synagogues, ¹¹ and a woman was there who had been crippled by a spirit for eighteen years. She was bent over and could not straighten up at all. ¹² When Jesus saw her, he called her forward and said to her, "Woman, you are set free from your infirmity." ¹³ Then he put his hands on her, and immediately she straightened up and praised God.

¹⁴ Indignant because Jesus had healed on the Sabbath, the synagogue leader said to the people, "There are six days for work. So come and be healed on those days, not on the Sabbath."

¹⁵ The Lord answered him, "You hypocrites! Doesn't each of you on the Sabbath untie your ox or donkey from the stall and lead it out to give it water? ¹⁶ Then should not this woman, a daughter of Abraham, whom Satan has kept bound for eighteen long years, be set free on the Sabbath day from what bound her?"

¹⁷ When he said this, all his opponents were humiliated, but the people were delighted with all the wonderful things he was doing.

The Sabbath day was one of the few ways in which the Jews of Jesus' time were able to distinguish themselves from other peoples on earth. Their strict observance of the Sabbath was an outward demonstration of their devotion to the one true God, Jehovah. Over the decades, they had developed many rules for observing the Sabbath.

All of these rules came about with the best intentions possible. They were honoring God. They needed to be observed. But eventually, the rules themselves had become sacred, particularly to the religious leaders of the nation.

Week 3: Finding Grace in Life's Hard Places

They were so sacred that they blinded the leaders of the synagogue to the good deeds that Jesus was doing and to his ultimate purpose on earth. Jesus was a rule-breaker, especially when the rules would prevent him from establishing the kingdom of God on earth.

This passage reminds us in this Lenten season that while rules, practices, and customs are important, none of these good things should get in the way of expressing our love for God and our fellow human beings. None of them should stop us from showing that love when and where we have the opportunity. The greatest commandments are to love God and to love our neighbors as ourselves. The rules, however good they are, should follow far behind those two commandments.

Let's pray: Our father, help us in our daily lives to see beyond the rules that we have set for ourselves and for others, and to catch a glimpse of your love and grace. Amen.

Grace for All podcast, episode 132

https://graceforall.captivate.fm/episode/rules-are-rules

Week 4: The Journey Home: A Pattern of Divine Reconciliation

Week 4: The Journey Home

Luke 15:11-32 NIV

11 Jesus continued: "There was a man who had two sons. 12 The younger one said to his father, 'Father, give me my share of the estate.' So he divided his property between them.

13 "Not long after that, the younger son got together all he had, set off for a distant country and there squandered his wealth in wild living. 14 After he had spent everything, there was a severe famine in that whole country, and he began to be in need. 15 So he went and hired himself out to a citizen of that country, who sent him to his fields to feed pigs. 16 He longed to fill his stomach with the pods that the pigs were eating, but no one gave him anything.

17 "When he came to his senses, he said, 'How many of my father's hired servants have food to spare, and here I am starving to death! 18 I will set out and go back to my father and say to him: Father, I have sinned against heaven and against you. 19 I am no longer worthy to be called your son; make me like one of your hired servants.' 20 So he got up and went to his father.

"But while he was still a long way off, his father saw him and was filled with compassion for him; he ran to his son, threw his arms around him and kissed him.

21 "The son said to him, 'Father, I have sinned against heaven and against you. I am no longer worthy to be called your son.'

22 "But the father said to his servants, 'Quick! Bring the best robe and put it on him. Put a ring on his finger and sandals on his feet. 23 Bring the fattened calf and kill it. Let's have a feast and celebrate. 24 For this son of mine was dead and is alive again; he was lost and is found.' So they began to celebrate.

25 "Meanwhile, the older son was in the field. When he came near the house, he heard music and dancing. 26 So he called one of the servants and asked him what was going on. 27 'Your brother has come,' he replied, 'and your father has killed the fattened calf because he has him back safe and sound.'

28 "The older brother became angry and refused to go in. So his father went out and pleaded with him. **29** But he answered his father, 'Look! All these years I've been slaving for you and never disobeyed your orders. Yet you never gave me even a young goat so I could celebrate with my friends. **30** But when this son of yours who has squandered your property with prostitutes comes home, you kill the fattened calf for him!'

31 "'My son,' the father said, 'you are always with me, and everything I have is yours. **32** But we had to celebrate and be glad, because this brother of yours was dead and is alive again; he was lost and is found.'"

Week 4: The Journey Home

A Divine Pattern

Have you ever taken a road trip and suddenly realized you're driving in the wrong direction? In the days before Google Maps and turn-by-turn guidance, many of us have mistakenly gone the wrong way more times than we care to admit. When you find yourself in that situation the only thing you can do is turn around and head in another direction.

That brings us to our theme today. Repentance literally means turning around. In this fourth lesson, we'll look at repentance and its close relative, reconciliation. Both are illustrated by stories – one ancient and the other quite contemporary. Both stories deal with tragic decisions and catastrophic consequences. However, as we have already seen in our study, God's grace meets us in our desperate lostness, calling us home.

When Grace Finds Us

The familiar story of the prodigal son reveals a pattern of repentance and reconciliation that still transforms lives today. We have read the ancient parable in the scripture for today, and we'll come back to that shortly. Now let's hear a real-life story of a difficult journey from repentance to reconciliation.

Meet Joe Avila, recovering alcoholic and ex-con.

Joe remembers the street sign not far from his house. It reads,

"Please do not drink and drive"

Beneath that sign is one that is smaller but no less important. It simply says,

"In honor of Amy Wall."

Joe's voice remains steady as he explains to the reporter interviewing him,

"Amy Wall was a young lady that I killed in 1992 while driving drunk on the freeway."

Like the prodigal son, Joe had wandered spiritually far from home. Among his many problems, his abuse of alcohol made his life worse. Driving drunk one night, Joe crashed his car into another driven by a teenage girl, Amy Wall.

When emergency crews arrived at the crash that night, Joe Avila had fled the scene. Firemen and medical teams worked quickly but it was too late. Theirs was the sad task of extracting Amy Wall's lifeless body from the tangle of twisted metal and broken glass.

The loss Amy's family bore was heartbreaking. Her brother lost his sister, and her parents their only daughter. They grieved her death, and with it the death of Amy's never-to-be-realized hopes, dreams, and possibilities. As anyone who has lost a child or close family member knows, grief can be suffocating. Even though the pain might ease some over time, there is never a moment when the loss is not felt.

The suffering Amy's family experienced cannot be compared to the accident's effect on Joe. His life would never be the same again, either, but he was alive. In jail, as he slowly emerged from his alcoholic haze, reality hit him. He had killed a teenage girl with his car. He had been apprehended and arrested. Officers had booked him into the Fresno County Jail, and he faced a second-degree murder charge. Distraught by what he had done, Joe considered suicide. "I was afraid, I was angry, I was sad," he recalls. But God wasn't finished with Joe's story yet.

While awaiting trial, Joe entered a six-month sobriety program. In counseling sessions, Joe heard for the first time that forgiveness and reconciliation were possible -- even for him. Like the prodigal "coming to himself" in the distant country, Joe reached a turning point. He decided his life needed to change.

Week 4: The Journey Home

Joe's "turn around" – his repentance – expressed itself, not just in feelings of remorse, but in redemptive action. Joe took full responsibility for his crime. Before his trial date in the spring of 1993, Joe changed his plea from not guilty to guilty. That step would become the first of many on his path to forgiveness and reconciliation.

The next seven and a half years in prison continued Joe's repentant journey of return. While incarcerated, he served hospice patients, maintained relationships with his daughters, and shared his renewed faith with fellow inmates. Inside the gray walls, Prison Fellowship became his new spiritual community. Outside, a local church encouraged Joe's restoration as a responsible member of the community.

When time came for his release from prison, Joe's support network marked his return to the community with yellow ribbons and a banner reading "Welcome Home, Joe!" Joe's long, difficult journey had finally brought him home again.

An Ancient Pattern Renewed

Joe's story is not unlike that of the prodigal son. When Jesus told that parable, his audience would have recognized a pattern woven throughout Israel's history -- rejection, repentance and reconciliation. The son's dramatic rejection of his father paralleled Israel's repeated turning away from God. His demand for his inheritance while his father still lived was just like saying, "I wish you were dead." It was a rejection not just of family, but of community, tradition, and his identity.

In addition, as Jesus told of the prodigal son's spiral downward, those hearing the story must have been shocked. A Jewish son feeding pigs -- unclean animals – was unimaginable and captured the depth of his fall. The son had not only left home; he had abandoned the faith practices that defined him.

The prodigal's moment of clarity -- "coming to himself" – would be mirrored again by Joe Avila's awakening in jail. Both men faced the stark reality of who they had become. Yet Jesus's parable emphasizes that recognition isn't enough. The son doesn't stop at awareness; he doesn't merely feel remorse. His pivotal words, "I will arise and go to my father," mark the need to both repent *and* return -- you cannot have one without the other.

The Father's Heart

However, even as he contemplates going back and groveling before his father, the son has no idea what has been happening at his home. His father has been watching for him every day. And, as soon as the father sees his lost son far away on the dusty road, he runs to greet him.

As Jesus described the father's response to the sight of his son, the audience must have been horrified. Middle Eastern patriarchs did not run -- it was considered undignified. Yet this father, seeing his son "while still far off," hikes up his robes and runs. Before the son can even apologize with his rehearsed speech, the father embraces him. He rallies the servants, calls for the best robe, a family ring, fresh sandals, and a feast of the best beef with all the trimmings.

Amazingly, the father's extravagant welcome finds its echo in the Wall family's remarkable grace toward Joe. Just as the prodigal's father took the initiative in reconciliation, Amy's brother, father, and mother asked to meet one-by-one with Joe. Through stories and tears, Joe experienced the family's heartbreak and sorrow. Yet, each family member helped Joe realize not only the pain his action had caused, but also the possibility his life still could realize.

And then, the day came when Rick Wall, Amy's father, extended love to the man whose carelessness had taken his daughter's life. Joe recalled the moment by saying, "Rick Wall, Amy's father, forgave me before I even asked him to forgive me," Joe recalls. One father dealing with his own loss, acted with the same love and forgiveness of the prodigal's father. And with the help of his community, his church, and the Wall family, Joe Avila finally found his way home.

The Challenge of the Elder Brother

Unfortunately, Jesus's parable doesn't end with the celebration, and neither does Joe's story. Real life is seldom neat and tidy. In Jesus's story, the older brother, who did not leave home, who faithfully served his father, and who did not receive a robe, a ring, a pair of sandals or a banquet, felt slighted. The elder brother's anger at his father's lavish welcome reminds us that some people struggle with the idea of showing grace, without reservation, to the undeserving.

Joe encountered similar resistance on his journey of restoration. Not everyone believed his transformation was genuine, including the judge who sentenced him.

Yet just as the father in the parable goes out to plead with his elder son, God's grace extends to both the obviously lost and the secretly estranged. The parable, like Joe's story, challenges us to examine which brother we most resemble -- the obvious sinner who repents, returns, and accepts grace, or the outwardly righteous one who struggles to celebrate restoration.

Living Reconciliation

Joe Avila's true story continues to inspire others. Joe still serves with Prison Fellowship, investing in others as people invested in him. His life demonstrates that genuine repentance bears fruit in action.

He explains his transformed life simply: "I wanted to honor my Lord and Savior Jesus Christ, and at the same time, I wanted to honor Amy and her life." His ongoing work mirrors the father's heart in Jesus's parable -- watching for the lost, running to meet them, and celebrating their return. His story, like the prodigal's, reminds us that true repentance helps us find our way home, again.

The Father Still Waits

This Lenten season invites us to examine our own lives. What would true repentance look like -- not just in feeling, but in action? The father in Jesus's parable and the Wall family in Joe's story remind us that reconciliation becomes possible when we turn our hearts toward home and take the first step of return. The father still watches, still runs to meet us, and still celebrates every child who was lost and but now is found.

Prayer

Gracious Father, give us courage not only to recognize our need to repent and return, but to begin the journey to come home to you. Help us trust in your boundless love that runs to meet us on the way. Amen.

Week 4: The Journey Home

Reflections for the week ahead

In this section, we have a combination of questions for reflection and devotional readings that provide personal insights designed to help you on your Lenten journey. The devotional readings are taken from the ***Grace for All*** podcast, a daily devotional podcast produced by the congregation of First United Methodist Church in Maryville, Tennessee.

We highly recommend listening and subscribing to this five-minute daily podcast. It can be found on the church website (https://1stchurch.org/extras/podcast) or on Apple Podcasts, Spotify, or anywhere you get your podcasts.

Monday: Where in your life have you wandered from God's path? What would concrete steps of return look like?

Tuesday: Read the devotion **"Love Your Enemies"** on the following pages. Who is your enemy? Do you agree with the conclusion of the writer of this devotion?

Wednesday: Reflect on times you've been like the elder brother, resistant to celebrating others' return. Ask God for the ability to see others as the Father sees them.

Thursday: Read the devotion **"Seize the Day"** on the following pages. Jesus wept, not over his fate but over the fate of those he loved but who had rejected him. What are the parallels between Jesus and the father of the two brothers?

Friday: Consider those who, like Joe, have helped you reconcile and forgive. Give thanks for their influence.

Saturday: Pray for those currently on the journey home, that they might find courage to face both life-changing transformation and a grace-filled return.

Tuesday Devotion: Love Your Enemies

Luke 6:27 NIV

But to you who are listening I say: Love your enemies, do good to those who hate you.

In reading this verse alone, without the context of the surrounding verses, I am at first reminded of the time, later in Luke (Chapter 10), where Jesus is questioned by a lawyer about the greatest of all commandments. Jesus asks the lawyer what he thinks. Love God and love your neighbor as yourself. Correct, says Jesus. But then the lawyer asks, "But who is my neighbor?" That question provides Jesus with the opportunity to relate possibly his most beautiful parable, the Good Samaritan.

In this passage, no one asks, "Who is my enemy?"

We don't have to ask. Many times in our lives, enemies surround us. We have no trouble identifying them. And therein lies the problem. We can, indeed, identify our enemies.

Jesus calls us not only to action but to "listen" and think deeply about what he is saying. If we do that, we may discover a hidden but essential truth. The person we love, because we love that person, can no longer be our enemy. We cannot identify that person as an enemy.

Yes, there may be those who "hate us." But we are not responsible for the feelings of another person. We are responsible for our own feelings and actions. If we follow this divine command, we will have no enemies.

Prayer: Loving God, show us how to follow your example, to love those who might hate us, to show love to those we might

Week 4: The Journey Home

consider enemies. Let us be transformed in Christ, that we might become friends to all the world. Amen.

Grace for All podcast, episode 103

https://graceforall.captivate.fm/episode/love-your-enemies

Thursday Devotion: Seize the Day

Luke 19:41-44 NIV

> *⁴¹As he approached Jerusalem and saw the city, he wept over it ⁴² and said, "If you, even you, had only known on this day what would bring you peace—but now it is hidden from your eyes. ⁴³ The days will come upon you when your enemies will build an embankment against you and encircle you and hem you in on every side. ⁴⁴ They will dash you to the ground, you and the children within your walls. They will not leave one stone on another, because you did not recognize the time of God's coming to you."*

We are told in many places in the scripture that God is always with us, that his presence is always there, no matter where we are, or what our circumstances are. Yet a very famous verse, says, seek the Lord while he may be found. It might lead us to ask, what's going on here? Is God really hiding his face from us?

This passage in the gospel of Luke tells us something that is very important and sheds light on what we might think is a contradiction. It takes us back to the short time before Christ's crucifixion, when he approaches the city of Jerusalem. He looks upon the city as a symbol of all of the people that he loves. If they had only recognized the time when he was close, when he was beside them, and responded to that.

But now it is too late. The people have hidden their eyes from him. They have missed their opportunity. Jesus was close by, in this case in the flesh, and they missed it.

These words provide us with the theme for our Grace for All podcasts over the next month. There are times in our lives when Jesus is particularly near. He is far away when we turn our eyes away from him, when we get distracted by our selfish

Week 4: The Journey Home

concerns, by the things that happen, by those things that seize our minds and attention, or just by everyday busyness of life.

Here we are reminded to recognize that God is with us, and that he is close to us. We must open our eyes and see him.

Our prayer today: dear Lord, help us always to be sensitive to your presence no matter where we are in life, no matter what has happened to us, no matter what the distractions are. We seek your presence, and we seek your closeness every day. Amen.

Grace for All podcast, episode 136

https://graceforall.captivate.fm/episode/seize-the-day

Week 5: The Fragrance of Love

Week 5: The Fragrance of Love

John 12:1-8 NIV

¹*Six days before the Passover, Jesus came to Bethany, where Lazarus lived, whom Jesus had raised from the dead.* ² *Here a dinner was given in Jesus' honor. Martha served, while Lazarus was among those reclining at the table with him.*

³ *Then Mary took about a pint of pure nard, an expensive perfume; she poured it on Jesus' feet and wiped his feet with her hair. And the house was filled with the fragrance of the perfume.*

⁴ *But one of his disciples, Judas Iscariot, who was later to betray him, objected,* ⁵ *"Why wasn't this perfume sold and the money given to the poor? It was worth a year's wages."* ⁶ *He did not say this because he cared about the poor but because he was a thief; as keeper of the money bag, he used to help himself to what was put into it.*

⁷ *"Leave her alone," Jesus replied. "It was intended that she should save this perfume for the day of my burial.* ⁸ *You will always have the poor among you, but you will not always have me."*

Sacred Moments

As our Lenten journey draws nearer to the crucifixion of Christ, we take a step back a few days before Palm Sunday to pause in Bethany for a dinner party. This is no ordinary gathering. Here in the home of Mary, Martha, and Lazarus, the aroma of celebration fills the banquet room. However, there are also subtle undertones of tension as an extraordinary act of devotion is about to unfold.

In the Home of Friends

Picture the scene: In a large upstairs space, thirteen men recline on cushioned couches arranged in a U-shape around low tables. They rest easily on their left elbows, their feet extending away from the tables, as was customary for such formal meals. Oil lamps cast flickering shadows on the walls. The mingled scents of lamb, fresh bread, and wine announce the evening's fare.

Jesus reclines in the place of honor. Near him is Lazarus – living proof of Jesus's power over death. Just days ago, Lazarus was dead and buried, four days in a tomb. There was no question Lazarus had died.

Now there is no doubt Lazarus is really alive because he is laughing and talking with the one who called him back to life. The twelve disciples fill the remaining places, companions whose conversations flow as easily as the wine.

Martha, always the hostess, moves efficiently between the kitchen and dining room, coordinating the courses of food with dutiful grace. The scene appears perfectly normal for a formal dinner party in the home of a well-to-do family, yet something electric hangs in the air. Those present can sense they are living an extraordinary drama.

Week 5: The Fragrance of Love

When Love Breaks Open

Quietly, Mary enters the room. Perhaps those closest to the doorway first notice the alabaster jar in her hands. After all, it was customary to bring scented water for guests to freshen their hands after the meal.

But something is different. As she approaches Jesus, the guest of honor, she does not offer him perfumed water to wash his hands. Instead, she moves away from the table, toward his feet. A few heads turn in her direction. But then she breaks the seal on the jar, and the potent fragrance of pure nard – far more costly than ordinary perfumes – cuts through the smell of dinner and wine.

We don't know for certain why Mary had such expensive burial spices on hand, but one intriguing possibility is that the nard was intended for Lazarus's burial. If so, imagine the profound symbolism: the very spices meant to prepare her brother for death, were rendered unnecessary by Jesus' life-giving power. Now Mary uses them for their new purpose -- to prepare Jesus for his own death.

As Mary continues, conversation in the room stops. All eyes are on Mary. With shocking immodesty, Mary lets down her hair, which proper Jewish women did not do in public. In the stunned silence, the clink of the alabaster jar lid, and the sound of perfume pouring out seems loud. All attention is fixed on her as she anoints Jesus's feet and then – incredibly – wipes them with her unbound hair.

Hearts Are Revealed

While the heavy scent of nard fills every corner of the room, something else fills the space as well – an uneasy tension. No one moves. Martha has paused her serving, a plate still in her hands. Lazarus watches his sister's act of devotion, understanding better than anyone the love that motivates it.

The disciples shift uncomfortably on their couches, embarrassed for Mary, but not certain how to respond to Mary's extravagant and intimate gesture.

Then Judas's insensitivity breaks the silence:

"Why wasn't this perfume sold and the money given to the poor?" he asked, his voice a little too strident.

His objection sounds reasonable, even pious. But its insincerity reveals something about his own spiritual condition.

Mary's action, shocking as it appears, flows from a heart that has been quietly cultivated through hours spent at Jesus's feet. On another occasion, Martha complained to Jesus because Mary wasn't helping her serve the guests. Instead, Mary was with the others, listening to Jesus.

Martha's protest then drew a gentle correction from Jesus. Hospitality was important, Jesus noted, but Mary had chosen the "better part." With Jesus's affirmation, future visits found Mary again with Jesus, listening, learning, and growing. Her spiritual sense continued to deepen through their relationship.

On the other hand, Judas's criticism, correct as it first sounds, emerges from a heart growing increasingly distant from Jesus. Judas is a future betrayer and a present thief, we are told. In contrast to Mary, his outward objection masks an inward spiritual decay.

The Master's Response

Jesus' words to Judas and the others – *"Leave her alone"* – do more than silence criticism. They validate what Mary's spiritual sensitivity has perceived. While others in the room are celebrating Lazarus' return to life, Mary has somehow grasped that Jesus is moving toward death.

Jesus continued to explain: *"It was intended that she should save this perfume for the day of my burial."*

Mary's extravagant gift, and her willingness to risk criticism and shame, flow from her deep insight. This is her gift to Jesus, her act of devotion that acknowledges their spiritual kinship.

A Lingering Fragrance

The nard's fragrance would have clung to Mary's hair for days. Long after the dinner party ended, she carried with her the scent of her devotion. We too experience its lingering fragrance as this story wafts across centuries to us. It carries a question as sharp and penetrating as the nard itself: How are we cultivating our spiritual perception?

The path to deeper spiritual sensitivity isn't mysterious. It is built through frequent decisions to draw near to Jesus, to listen, and to let our hearts be shaped by his presence.

Mary's extravagant act flowed naturally from a heart attuned to Jesus through relationship. Her spiritual sensitivity wasn't achieved in one moment, but developed through her ongoing choice to be present with Jesus.

While Jesus is no longer physically present with us, we can perform our own acts of devotion to Christ as bold as Mary's. Acts that reveal our own spiritual perception because we have spent time with Jesus ourselves. And when we do, the scent of those deeds will linger on us, reminding us of the fragrance of love.

Prayer

Lord Jesus, help us to cultivate spiritual insight through genuine relationship with you. Give us hearts that are sensitive to your presence and your leading, and the courage to respond in love, whatever others might think. Amen.

Reflections for the week ahead

In this section, we have a combination of questions for reflection and devotional readings that provide personal insights designed to help you on your Lenten journey. The devotional readings are taken from the ***Grace for All*** podcast, a daily devotional podcast produced by the congregation of First United Methodist Church in Maryville, Tennessee.

We highly recommend listening and subscribing to this five-minute daily podcast. It can be found on the [church website](https://1stchurch.org/extras/podcast) (https://1stchurch.org/extras/podcast) or on Apple Podcasts, Spotify, or anywhere you get your podcasts.

Monday: Sit quietly for a few minutes, asking God to help you notice where your heart may have grown distant from Jesus.

Tuesday: Read the devotion **"No More Excuses"** on the following pages. How does the passage of scripture in this devotion speak to you and the excuses you are using.

Wednesday: Reflect on times when you've felt the sting of criticism or the embarrassment of "overdoing" your devotion to Jesus. How did Jesus's defense of Mary encourage you?

Thursday: Read the devotion **"Where are You Planted?"** on the following pages. Do you hide away from the opportunities that God gives you to show his kindness and love?

Friday: Spend time today simply "sitting at Jesus's feet" through scripture and prayer, cultivating spiritual perception.

Saturday: Consider how your relationship with Jesus shapes how you see the moments of your life. Ask for greater sensitivity to his presence and purpose.

Week 5: The Fragrance of Love

Tuesday Devotion: No More Excuses

Isaiah 1:10, 16–20 NRSV

[10] Hear the word of the Lord, you rulers of Sodom! Listen to the teaching of our God, you people of Gomorrah!

[16] Wash yourselves; make yourselves clean; remove the evil of your doings from before my eyes; cease to do evil, [17] learn to do good; Seek justice, rescue the oppressed, defend the orphan, plead for the widow.

[18] Come, now, let us argue it out, says the Lord: though your sins are like scarlet, they should be like snow; though they are red like crimson, they should become like wool.

[19] If you are willing and obedient, you shall eat the good things of the land; [20] but if you refuse and rebel, you shall be devoured by the sword; for the mouth of the Lord has spoken.

During the four decades, during which I was a college professor, I heard all of the excuses. Students could not come to class, could not complete their assignments, could not do the things that they were supposed to do and that I knew that they could do all because of… well, you could fill in the blank. Numerous times, I asked the students, no matter what their failings, to stop offering me excuses. The excuses did me no good, and they were certainly not doing the students any good. And yet, the excuses continued no matter how much I asked them to stop.

In truth, however, I am no better than many of my students. I am an expert at making excuses for myself. There is always a reason why I can't do as I should. I have a whole list: That's the way I am. That's the way my parents raised me. I don't have it in me. I don't know how.

In this passage of scripture, God, speaking through the prophet Isaiah, is clear and refreshingly direct. If anything, he sounds a little like an exasperated teacher. No more excuses. Wash yourselves and make yourselves clean. Remove the evil things from your life. Do the right thing.

If there is something that we need to talk about, God says, then let's talk. Let's argue it out. It is a direct challenge to all of our excuses. If I get into an argument with God, I'm pretty sure I know who's going to win that one.

And then God offers us a promise, a promise of forgiveness. If we will do the things that he asks, our sins will be washed away. What thing on earth can we want more than to have our sins forgiven, to be in the presence of the God who loves us, and to know his spirit and his grace more fully? What excuse can we offer for rejecting that?

Our Father, help us to accept the commandment to put aside our excuses so that you can forgive our sins and that we can experience your love and grace. Amen.

Grace for All podcast, episode 153

https://graceforall.captivate.fm/episode/no-more-excuses

Week 5: The Fragrance of Love

Thursday Devotion: Where are You Planted?

Jeremiah 17: 5–8 NIV

⁵*This is what the Lord says: "Cursed is the one who trusts in man, who draws strength from mere flesh, and whose heart turned away from the Lord.*

⁶*That person will be like a bush in the wasteland. They will not see prosperity when it comes. They will dwell in the parched places of the desert, in a salt land where no one lives.*

⁷*But blessed is the one who trusts in the Lord, whose confidence is in him.*

⁸*They will be like a tree planted by the water that sends out its roots by the stream. It does not fear when heat comes; its leaves are always green. It has no worries in a year of drought and never fails to bear fruit."*

All of us are accidents of geography. We do not choose where we are born or where in our early lives we live. Some people grow up in fairly stable and unchanging environments. Others are shifted from place to place on a regular basis.

Even in our adult lives, we often feel like we have little choice about where we are. We're in a certain place because that's where the job opportunities exist. We locate in a certain city, because family or friends are there. We do not always get a choice about where we land.

Our spiritual lives are something else, however. In that realm, we can choose where we are planted. This passage in Jeremiah uses a very familiar analogy to ask a central question about our spiritual lives: Where do you choose to be planted?

Do you choose a desert environment, a place where there is little water and sustenance for you to grow? The Lord, speaking through Jeremiah, says that you can be like a bush planted in the desert, barely surviving and bearing no fruit.

Or you can choose to plant yourself by a stream and to sink your roots deep into that ground. You can grow to where you are unafraid of the drought or the high winds. You can bear fruit no matter what the conditions because your roots are deep and your branches are strong. This is your choice, your decision to make.

Where are you planted?

Our Father, guide me in the choices I make about where I should plant myself. Help me to find a place by your living water, to sink my roots deeply, and to bear fruit for your kingdom. Amen.

Grace for All podcast, episode 277

https://graceforall.captivate.fm/episode/where-are-you-planted

Week 6: A Tale of Two Kingdoms

Week 6: A Tale of Two Kingdoms

Luke 19:28-40 NIV

28 After Jesus had said this, he went on ahead, going up to Jerusalem. 29 As he approached Bethphage and Bethany at the hill called the Mount of Olives, he sent two of his disciples, saying to them, 30 "Go to the village ahead of you, and as you enter it, you will find a colt tied there, which no one has ever ridden. Untie it and bring it here. 31 If anyone asks you, 'Why are you untying it?' say, 'The Lord needs it.'"

32 Those who were sent ahead went and found it just as he had told them. 33 As they were untying the colt, its owners asked them, "Why are you untying the colt?"

34 They replied, "The Lord needs it."

35 They brought it to Jesus, threw their cloaks on the colt and put Jesus on it. 36 As he went along, people spread their cloaks on the road.

37 When he came near the place where the road goes down the Mount of Olives, the whole crowd of disciples began joyfully to praise God in loud voices for all the miracles they had seen:

38 "Blessed is the king who comes in the name of the Lord!"[a]

"Peace in heaven and glory in the highest!"

39 Some of the Pharisees in the crowd said to Jesus, "Teacher, rebuke your disciples!"

40 "I tell you," he replied, "if they keep quiet, the stones will cry out."

Week 6: A Tale of Two Kingdoms

When Kingdoms Collide

As we enter Holy Week, we stand at a crossroads – not just in the church calendar, but in our understanding of what it means to follow Jesus. Palm Sunday presents us with a profound choice, one that echoes through the centuries to challenge us today. What kind of king do we expect? What kind of kingdom are we looking for?

A Day of Two Parades

Imagine standing in Jerusalem 2,000 years ago. Passover week is upon us, and the city already is buzzing with anticipation. Pilgrims continue to flood into Jerusalem for the Passover festivities, centered in the Temple. But this morning, as the rising sun bathes the ancient city walls in golden light, something else is stirring. Two very different processions are approaching this holy city.*

From the western gate comes the thundering sound of hoofbeats and the rhythmic clang of metal on metal. Projecting an aura of invincibility, Pontius Pilate, the Roman governor, leads his troops into Jerusalem in a calculated display of imperial might.

Swaying above the column of soldiers, bronze eagles gleam atop their military standards. This symbol of Rome's supreme power is being deliberately paraded through the sacred city. The sight of these foreign emblems makes bystanders turn away in disgust and anger. To many Jews, the bronze eagles are an offense against the commandments.

---

* Two such processions are described in The Last Week: What the Gospels Really Teach About Jesus' Last Days in Jerusalem, *Marcus Borg and John Dominic Crossan. Harper One Reprint edition, 2007*

The crowds scatter as the procession pushes its way through the narrow streets toward Antonia's Fortress, Pilate's headquarters. The fortress looms over the Temple complex, a massive stone reminder of Roman dominance. From there, Pilate literally can look down on the Jews as they remember the story of God liberating them from slavery.

Pilate commands about 5,000 Roman soldiers in Judea. Antonia's Fortress houses about 500 normally, and Pilate's contingent will add to their number during Passover. This force, armed and alert, would quickly suppress any spontaneous insurrection. Although centuries have passed since the Exodus, Pilate is keenly aware that Passover could again stir hope among the Jews of freedom from oppressors.

As Pilate's parade passes, centuries of Roman military discipline are evident – organized, prepared, overwhelming. This is raw Roman power on display in Jerusalem, warning against uprising.

In contrast, from the east, a very different procession winds its way down the Mount of Olives.

There are no trumpets to announce this parade, no standards of national power, no steeds of war, no armored legionnaires marching in lockstep.

Instead, the dirt path bears the clop-clop of a young donkey's hooves. Sitting astride the animal on a makeshift saddle of cloaks and robes rides Jesus.

The rag-tag crowd, walking and dancing around Jesus' and his donkey, waves palm branches. Men and women, little children, and Jesus' band of disciples all flow together toward the city of Jerusalem.

As gestures of both affection and honor, men shed their cloaks to lay in Jesus' path, while women and children strow flowers and palm branches. Joy and singing, laughter and shouts of

Week 6: A Tale of Two Kingdoms

praise radiate from this moving mass of humanity with Jesus at its center. The palms and the people echo the ancient songs of God in their midst.

The peasant parade sings as it surges toward Jerusalem, and their songs are the words of the psalms: "Hosanna! Blessed is he who comes in the name of the Lord!"

The crowd's choruses invoke the hope of David's kingdom, as their voices rise with pent-up emotion. Children dart in and out of the procession, adding their innocent delight to the jubilant chaos. Unlike Pilate's carefully choreographed display, this spontaneous procession is driven by joy and hope.

The contrasts are evident: Jesus chooses to ride a donkey, instead of a war horse, in conscious fulfillment of Zechariah's prophecy about a king of peace. Pilate's procession moves toward Antonia's Fortress to lord it over the Temple, but Jesus' path will take him into the Temple itself. His intent there is not to dominate the Temple, but to cleanse it and restore its true purpose as a house of prayer for all nations.

Jerusalem at the Crossroads

In Jerusalem, the holy city has chafed under Roman occupation. Like any occupied nation, the Jews had not forgotten their history. They had once been free and had governed themselves. And they did remember how, after losing that freedom for 400-years, their ancestors had been liberated from Egypt during that first Passover. Now, as thousands of pilgrims flooded the city for the festival, the air was electric with possibility and tension.

The Romans knew this history too. They remembered another Jewish uprising after Herod's death in 4 BC, which had started in nearby Sepphoris and spread like wildfire. Their response had been swift and brutal. Once the rebellion was quashed, Pilate ordered the public crucifixion of over 2,000 rebels as a

> **Just as those ancient witnesses had to choose between the two processions, today we face a similar choice. Two contrasting visions compete for our attention each day in the news, on our screens, and in our culture.**

warning to others. Now, during Passover, Pilate ratcheted up the military presence in Jerusalem. His procession was both a show of force and a warning: Rome was watching.

Into this powder keg of political and religious tension, Jesus deliberately chose to enter Jerusalem in a way that recalled the ancient prophecy of Zechariah: "See, your king comes to you, righteous and victorious, lowly and riding on a donkey" (Zechariah 9:9). This was no accident. Every detail of Jesus' entry was carefully chosen to present a divine vision of God's kingdom.

Two processions enter Jerusalem. One projects its message of violence and intimidation. The other sings of peace and freedom.

One offers the Pax Romana – peace at the point of a sword. The other proclaims Shalom Adonai – the peace of the Lord. Two kingdoms, two visions of power, two utterly incompatible ways of changing the world.

The King Who Disappoints

The crowd that welcomed Jesus understood the symbolism of his entry – or at least they thought they did. They cried "Hosanna to the Son of David!" believing that here, at last, was the descendant of David, who would restore Israel's glory. Just as David defeated Goliath, they thought, Jesus would drive out the Empire's occupiers and establish God's kingdom now.

But the hopes of desperate people are often self-serving, and their expectations wishful thinking. Jesus would be a king like David, but not the warrior. Instead, Jesus would personify the man after God's own heart. His kingdom would be an eternal kingdom, but not one secured through military might or political power. The peace he offered wasn't backed by legions of soldiers but by sacrificial love. The victory he sought wouldn't be achieved by killing enemies but by loving and dying for them.

This is why, by the end of the week, the crowds would turn against him. He had failed to be the kind of king they wanted. Instead of rallying an army, he cleared the Temple. Instead of plotting military strategy, he taught about loving enemies. Instead of stockpiling weapons, he broke bread with his followers and washed their feet.

Choosing Our Kingdom

Just as those ancient witnesses had to choose between the two processions, today we face a similar choice. Two contrasting visions compete for our attention each day in the news, on our screens, and in our culture. One offers the allure of power, success, and control. It comes with impressive credentials, convincing arguments, and promises of security and influence. Its drums beat out an insistent rhythm: "This is how the world works. This is how you get things done. This is how you win."

The other vision looks foolish by worldly standards. It comes in humility, offering a different kind of power – the power of love, service, and sacrifice. It invites us to follow a king whose standard is a cross, who wins through surrender, who shows strength through weakness.

Which Parade Are You Following?

As we enter Holy Week, the question echoes down the centuries: Which procession will we join? Will we follow the crowds cozying up to real world power and success? Or will we follow Jesus on the path that leads through sacrifice and suffering into the presence of God?

The choice is ours. The two paths lead to very different destinations. One leads to a kingdom that must be kept by force and violence. The other leads to the cross -- and through it, to resurrection.

Prayer

Lord Jesus, give us courage to choose your kingdom over the kingdoms of this world, even when your way seems foolish by worldly standards. Help us follow you on the path of humble service and self-giving love. Amen.

Week 6: A Tale of Two Kingdoms

Reflections for the week ahead

In this section, we have a combination of questions for reflection and devotional readings that provide personal insights designed to help you on your Lenten journey. The devotional readings are taken from the **Grace for All** podcast, a daily devotional podcast produced by the congregation of First United Methodist Church in Maryville, Tennessee.

We highly recommend listening and subscribing to this five-minute daily podcast. It can be found on the church website (https://1stchurch.org/extras/podcast) or on Apple Podcasts, Spotify, or anywhere you get your podcasts.

Monday: Notice where you're tempted to choose power over humility today. How might Jesus' example challenge these impulses?

Tuesday: Read the devotion **"Fear Not Your Inadequacies"** on the following pages. What are the problems you face that you simply cannot overcome? Are they too big, even for God?

Wednesday: Consider a situation where God's ways have disappointed your expectations. What might God be teaching you through this?

Thursday: Read the devotion **"Good News"** on the following pages. Are you someone who gets overwhelmed by the bad news of the day? Do you remind yourself that the gospel is good news?

Friday: Meditate on Jesus' choice to embrace weakness rather than worldly power. How does this challenge your own choices?

Saturday: As Holy Week approaches, prepare your heart to follow Jesus through death to resurrection. What needs to die in you so that Christ's life can be revealed?

Tuesday Devotion: Fear Not Your Inadequacies

John 6:5-9 NIV

> *⁵When Jesus looked up and saw a great crowd coming toward him, he said to Philip, "Where shall we buy bread for these people to eat?" ⁶ He asked this only to test him, for he already had in mind what he was going to do.*
>
> *⁷ Philip answered him, "It would take more than half a year's wages[a] to buy enough bread for each one to have a bite!"*
>
> *⁸ Another of his disciples, Andrew, Simon Peter's brother, spoke up,⁹ "Here is a boy with five small barley loaves and two small fish, but how far will they go among so many?"*

This is the famous story of Jesus and his disciples feeding the 5,000, the crowd that had gathered around Jesus. It appears in all four of the gospels, but in the verses we just read, we don't hear the end of the story. We should pay attention to the way in which this story develops.

The problem is enormous. Five thousand people need to be fed. Jesus asked Philip what he should do, and Philip, typical of the disciples and typical of many of us, simply describes the problem. A half a year's wages would not feed all of these people adequately.

Another disciple, Andrew, brings to Jesus a small boy who has only five loaves and two fish, and Andrew is quick to point out how little this is compared to the problem that they face.

We face enormous problems. Wars and cruelties surround us. Climate change is upon us. Our political and social systems are wracked with division. Even the church has problems that seem insurmountable. And we have so little to offer. Our resources are totally inadequate, and, as shown here, there are always people who are willing to point that out.

We fear that we cannot solve these problems, and the temptation for us is to give up.

It is certainly true that in facing many of our problems, both personal and social, we lack the resources to solve them or even to make much difference. But then we remember what happened in this particular story. Jesus took the bread and the fish that the little boy had brought and blessed it. And after that, in a short amount of time, everyone in that multitude was fed and satisfied, and there was food leftover.

In facing the problems that we have today, what if we simply presented the small resources that we have or did the inadequate things that we could do, and then we asked Jesus to bless those things. What do you think might happen?

Would you pray with me? Our Father, we do not need to be reminded that our resources and efforts are totally inadequate to solve many of the problems that we face. We do need to be reminded of your power and your grace and the way it works in all situations. Help us to rely not on the resources that we have but on the abilities and resources of your spirit. Amen.

Grace for All podcast, episode 203

https://graceforall.captivate.fm/episode/fear-not-your-inadequacies

Thursday Devotion: Good News

Mark 1:12-15 NIV

> [12] At once the Spirit sent him out into the wilderness, [13] and he was in the wilderness forty days, being tempted[a] by Satan. He was with the wild animals, and angels attended him.
>
> [14] After John was put in prison, Jesus went into Galilee, proclaiming the good news of God. [15] "The time has come," he said. "The kingdom of God has come near. Repent and believe the good news!"

From the time that I was a teenager, I wanted to be a journalist. I was able to fulfill that ambition, first as a news reporter and editor later as a journalism educator. During my teaching career, I tried to give students some instruction on the basic techniques and tenets of journalism. One of those tenets was to try, as much as humanly possible, to be accurate in the reporting of news. What you want, I would tell them, is for people to believe what you report.

As a journalist and journalist educator, it has meant something special to me that the gospel is described as "good news." All of us know that there is a lot of bad news in our world today. The bad news can overwhelm us.

Indeed, some people not only believe the bad news, but they believe **IN** the bad news. They believe that the world is doomed, and that we are condemned to be consumed, either by environmental catastrophe or apocalyptic war. There is simply no hope for the world.

In this passage in the gospel of Mark, Jesus tells us something very different. The kingdom of God is at hand, he says. He has good news, and we are to believe *in* that good news. Yes, there

Week 6: A Tale of Two Kingdoms

is plenty of bad news in our world today. We believe that bad news. But Jesus has given us good news, *the* good news of God's love and grace. While we believe the bad news, we can believe **IN** the good news of the kingdom of God.

Our prayer today: Our Father, with all of the bad news around us each day, help us to keep our eyes focused on the good news of your kingdom, your grace, and your love. Amen.

Grace for All podcast, episode 221

https://graceforall.captivate.fm/episode/good-news

Week 7: When You Are Looking for Jesus: A Resurrection Story

Week 7: When You Are Looking for Jesus

Luke 24:1-12 NIV

¹On the first day of the week, very early in the morning, the women took the spices they had prepared and went to the tomb.

² They found the stone rolled away from the tomb,

³ but when they entered, they did not find the body of the Lord Jesus.

⁴ While they were wondering about this, suddenly two men in clothes that gleamed like lightning stood beside them.

⁵ In their fright the women bowed down with their faces to the ground, but the men said to them, "Why do you look for the living among the dead?

⁶ He is not here; he has risen! Remember how he told you, while he was still with you in Galilee:

⁷ 'The Son of Man must be delivered over to the hands of sinners, be crucified and on the third day be raised again.' "

⁸ Then they remembered his words.

⁹ When they came back from the tomb, they told all these things to the Eleven and to all the others.

¹⁰ It was Mary Magdalene, Joanna, Mary the mother of James, and the others with them who told this to the apostles.

¹¹ But they did not believe the women, because their words seemed to them like nonsense.

¹² Peter, however, got up and ran to the tomb. Bending over, he saw the strips of linen lying by themselves, and he went away, wondering to himself what had happened.

The Day We Lost Our Young Daughter...Briefly

Nothing strikes panic in a parent's heart like losing sight of their child. I learned this firsthand one summer afternoon when our three-year-old daughter Laurie disappeared from our parsonage home in rural Georgia.

My wife Debbie had just settled our newborn Amy down when she realized the house had grown too quiet - that eerie silence that parents know means trouble. A quick search through our small house yielded no sign of Laurie. Debbie's heart began racing as she rushed outside, calling Laurie's name.

As she rounded the corner of the house, Debbie spotted our determined little daughter running full-speed toward the neighbor's house, which was on the other side of a dirt road - a road frequently used by fast-moving farm trucks. Debbie sprinted after her, managing to catch her by the back of her shirt just steps from the road's edge.

"Where are you going?" Debbie asked, trying to catch her breath.

"I'm going to get a hot dog! I know the way!" came Laurie's confident reply. We had enjoyed hot dogs at the neighbor's house the day before, and our independent three-year-old had decided to make a return visit - alone.

That moment of panic, followed by profound relief, comes back to me every time I read about that first Easter morning. Just as Debbie frantically searched for our daughter, a group of women made their way to Jesus' tomb before dawn, hearts heavy with grief. They knew exactly where they had laid his body - or so they thought. But like my daughter's momentary disappearance, the women were about to discover that Jesus wasn't where they expected him to be.

Week 7: When You Are Looking for Jesus

Looking for Jesus in the Wrong Place

Just like we were searching for our daughter in all the familiar places that morning, a group of women made their way through the pre-dawn darkness to find Jesus. They knew exactly where to look - the tomb of Joseph of Arimathea where they had watched others lay Jesus' body just days before. They came carrying spices to properly prepare his body, a task left undone in the rush to beat sundown and the Sabbath on that terrible Friday.

But what these faithful women found - or rather didn't find - sent their hearts racing. The massive stone that had sealed the tomb was rolled away. Cautiously entering the dark chamber, they discovered Jesus' body was gone.

These women stood in stunned silence, trying to make sense of an empty tomb. Their confusion quickly turned to terror when two men in dazzling clothes suddenly appeared beside them. The women fell to the ground, shielding their eyes from the heavenly brightness.

Then came the angels' gentle rebuke that would forever change how we think about where to find Jesus: "Why do you look for the living among the dead? He is not here; he has risen!"

The angels reminded them of Jesus' own words - how he had told them he would be handed over to sinners, be crucified, and rise again on the third day. Like all of us when confronted with the unexpected, the women had forgotten these promises in their grief and confusion. But now, standing in that empty tomb, Jesus' words came rushing back.

The biblical story of the women at the tomb provides a guide for us as we seek the living Christ's presence, but sometimes do not know where to look. Let's explore three insights we can glean from this story of the women who were looking for Jesus.

First, when you are looking for Jesus, look in the right place.

Like those women at the tomb, we often look for Jesus where we last saw him, where we expect him to be. The angels' gentle rebuke - "Why do you look for the living among the dead?" - challenges us to expand our vision. Where should we look? Jesus himself showed us - in the streets where he taught, beside the beds of the sick, at dinner tables with those society rejected, among the poor and forgotten. Even now, Jesus is more likely to be found in a homeless shelter than a palace, in a prison ministry than a private golf club.

When my wife found our daughter that morning, Laurie wasn't lost - she knew exactly where she was going. Similarly, Jesus wasn't lost - he was exactly where he said he would be, doing what he said he would do. The challenge isn't finding Jesus; it's adjusting our expectations about where to look.

Second, when looking for Jesus, listen to those who love him.

The women at the tomb - Mary Magdalene, Joanna, Mary the mother of James, and others - were Jesus' devoted followers. They supported his ministry, listened to his teaching, and remained faithful even at the cross when others fled. When they reported the empty tomb to the disciples, the all-male group didn't listen to the women, dismissing their testimony as "nonsense." But the fact that the Gospel writers later included the women's testimony – and the disciples' mistake – indicates that the early church valued the women's witness to the resurrection.

Today, if you want to find Jesus, spend time with those who love him deeply - not just those who talk about him the most. Look for the quiet servants, like the women, who feed the hungry, visit the sick, and offer hospitality to others. They often

Week 7: When You Are Looking for Jesus

know where to find Jesus because they've spent time walking where he walks.

Third, when looking for Jesus, learn to recognize the clues of his presence.

Peter later ran to the tomb and saw the linen cloths lying there - a clue that something extraordinary had occurred. But like many of us, he went away "wondering what had happened." Sometimes we miss Jesus because we're looking for dramatic signs when instead he often leaves subtle clues. A word of encouragement from a stranger, an unexpected act of kindness, or a moment of grace when we are struggling can act as hints of Jesus' unexpected presence.

Our daughter's predictable love of hot dogs led her straight to our neighbor's house on that summer morning. Believe it or not, Jesus is equally predictable. You'll find him where his heart has always led him - where people are hurting, where grace is needed, where love is being shared. The clues are there if we learn to recognize them.

Finding Jesus Today

That morning years ago when we found our daughter heading determinedly toward what she wanted, I learned something about looking in the right places. We can know where to find Jesus if we understand what has always drawn him – the outcasts, those hurting, and those searching.

The women who came to the tomb that first Easter morning had to adjust their expectations. They came looking for a dead teacher and found instead evidence of the risen Lord. We too must often adjust our expectations, learning to see Jesus not just where we assume he is, but in the challenging places where his love is most needed.

Like those faithful women, we're called to be witnesses to Christ's risen presence in our world. We may not see angels in dazzling clothes, but if we know where to look, we can see Jesus at work in the everyday miracles of changed lives, restored relationships, and sacrificial love.

Let us pray:

Risen Lord, open our eyes to see you in unexpected places. Give us hearts to recognize your presence in those who serve quietly and faithfully. Help us not to look for you only where we assume you are, but to follow where you lead, even when it surprises us. Thank you that you are not dead but alive, not distant but present, not lost but always findable by those who seek you with their whole hearts. Amen.

Week 7: When You Are Looking for Jesus

Reflections for the week ahead

In this section, we have a combination of questions for reflection and devotional readings that provide personal insights designed to help you on your Lenten journey. The devotional readings are taken from the ***Grace for All*** podcast, a daily devotional podcast produced by the congregation of First United Methodist Church in Maryville, Tennessee.

We highly recommend listening and subscribing to this five-minute daily podcast. It can be found on the [church website](https://1stchurch.org/extras/podcast) (https://1stchurch.org/extras/podcast) or on Apple Podcasts, Spotify, or anywhere you get your podcasts.

Monday: "Why do you look for the living among the dead?" Where might you be looking for Jesus in places or ways that no longer hold life?

Tuesday: Read the devotion **"Fear and Understanding"** on the following pages. How does "fearing" God deepen our understanding of what Christ's followers found on that Easter morning?

Wednesday: What "clues" of Jesus' presence have you noticed in your daily life this week? How might you become more attentive to these signs?

Thursday: Read the devotion **"Whither Shall We Go."** Can we ever dismiss ourselves from God's presence?

Friday: The disciples initially dismissed the women's testimony. When have you perhaps dismissed an unlikely messenger of God's truth?

Saturday: The women came prepared to tend Jesus' body but instead found new life. How might God be turning your expressions of faithful service into unexpected encounters with the living Christ?

Tuesday Devotion: Fear and Understanding

Proverbs 9:10 NIV
The fear of the LORD is the beginning of wisdom, and knowledge of the Holy One is understanding.

Scripture teaches us to "Fear not." We are not to fear others who oppose us. We are not to fear dangerous situations. We are not to fear the future. We are to put our trust in God.

And so we should. But these passages of scripture do not mean that we should put aside the emotion of fear completely.

A positive side of fear is that it makes us pay attention and to focus on what is in front of us and important to us.

That is what the writer of Proverbs is getting at in this verse.

In some translations of this passage, we see the word "fear" substituted with words like "respect" or "reverence." These are legitimate meanings, but for me they fall short of the depths that the word "fear."

The power and might of God are awesome things to behold. They should engender in us some level of fear.

We should not stop with just fear. That fear should lead us somewhere. It should lead us to an understanding of the Almighty. It is, in the words of the proverbist, "the beginning of wisdom."

While I will never in this life understand the enormity of God's love, power and grace, I want to come as close to that understanding as possible.

The fear of the Lord is where I must begin that journey.

Week 7: When You Are Looking for Jesus

Prayer

Our Father, my prayer each day is to increase my understanding of the depths of your love and grace, Amen.

Grace for All podcast, episode 212

https://graceforall.captivate.fm/episode/whither-shall-we-go

Thursday Devotion: Whither Shall We Go

Psalms 139:7-12 NIV

> *⁷Where can I go from your Spirit?*
> *Where can I flee from your presence?*
> *⁸ If I go up to the heavens, you are there;*
> *if I make my bed in the depths, you are there.*
> *⁹ If I rise on the wings of the dawn,*
> *if I settle on the far side of the sea,*
> *¹⁰ even there your hand will guide me,*
> *your right hand will hold me fast.*
> *¹¹ If I say, "Surely the darkness will hide me*
> *and the light become night around me,"*
> *¹² even the darkness will not be dark to you;*
> *the night will shine like the day,*
> *for darkness is as light to you.*

Not long ago, a bumper sticker caught my eye. It read: "God doesn't believe in atheists." That statement made me pause, ponder its intent, and ultimately conclude it was a clever but narrow-minded view of people. My gut reaction was:

You know, God *does* believe in atheists.

In the passage we just read, the Psalmist presents a range of choices for directing our lives. We can ascend to heaven, make our bed in hell, or fly to the distant reaches of the sea. Yet, wherever we are, even if we summon darkness to engulf us, God remains present. Some may declare their disbelief in God throughout their lives, attempting to persuade others to think and act as if God never existed, as if creation somehow spontaneously arose.

These reminders in the Psalms serve as a powerful message: our attempts to distance ourselves from God are ultimately futile. Nothing we say or no place we go can remove us from His presence. He is always with us, at our right hand, ready to offer his grace and love. No matter who we are, what we say, or where we choose to be, God believes in us. And he is always there.

Prayer

Dear Lord, thank you for the constant assurance of your presence, regardless of what we say about you or where we choose to be. You are always there, and for that, our hearts overflow with gratitude. Amen.

Grace for All podcast, episode 264

https://graceforall.captivate.fm/episode/whither-shall-we-go

Introduction to the Leader's Guide

This Leader's Guide is designed to help you facilitate meaningful group study and discussion of *"The Way of Grace"* during the season of Lent. The guide provides a flexible framework that can be used by both Sunday morning classes and weekday study groups.

Teaching Schedule

The study follows seven key biblical passages from Ash Wednesday through Easter Sunday. Each week's session builds upon the previous ones, creating a progressive journey through Lent. The core teaching time is structured for 50 minutes.

Understanding the Guide Format

Each week's session includes these core components:

Opening (7 minutes)

Begin with welcome and prayer, followed by a brief check-in about participants' experiences with the previous week's reflections. This sets the tone for open, honest discussion.

Scripture Engagement (12 minutes)

Choose from several suggested methods for reading and engaging with the week's passage. Whether through dramatic reading, Lectio Divina, or group reading patterns, this component helps participants encounter the text in fresh ways.

Essential Context (8 minutes)

Leader's Guide

Present key historical, cultural, and theological background that illuminates the passage. This brief overview provides context while maintaining focus on personal application.

Group Discussion (15 minutes)

Guide conversation using provided questions that connect the text to contemporary life. This is the heart of each session, where participants wrestle with meaning and application.

Closing Integration (8 minutes)

Wrap up with preview of next week's theme, review of daily reflections, and closing prayer. This component helps participants carry the lesson's insights into their week.

Adapting the Material

While this guide provides structured plans and resources, you know your group best. Feel free to modify the suggested formats, timing, and activities to match your group's:

- Size and dynamics

- Biblical knowledge level

- Learning preferences

- Time constraints

- Spiritual maturity

- Discussion style

The most effective small group leaders are those who use guides like this as a resource rather than a rigid script. Trust your experience with your group to know when to probe deeper, when to move on, and how to make the material most meaningful for your specific context.

Remember, the goal isn't to cover every suggested activity or question, but to facilitate genuine engagement with Scripture and meaningful spiritual growth during this Lenten season. Let the Holy Spirit guide your leadership as you journey with your group through these powerful Gospel passages.

Week 1 Leader's Guide: Our Lenten Journey Begins with a Test

(Luke 4:1-13)

Core Session Components (50 minutes)

Opening (7 minutes)

- Welcome to the beginning of our Lenten journey
- Opening Prayer
- Check-in question: "When have you felt tested in your faith journey?"
- Link to Lenten themes of preparation and spiritual growth

Scripture Engagement (12 minutes)

Choose ONE method:

1. **Desert Voices**
   - Narrator: reads descriptive parts
   - Jesus: reads responses
   - Satan: reads temptations
   - Pay attention to the progression of testing

2. Wilderness Reading

- Read passage twice slowly
- First reading: Focus on physical setting and circumstances
- Second reading: Notice spiritual and emotional dynamics
- Share what stands out in each reading

Essential Context (8 minutes)

The forty days Jesus spent in the wilderness echo Israel's forty years of desert wandering, but with a crucial difference. Where Israel frequently failed their tests of faith, Jesus remained faithful. The desert itself held deep significance in Jewish spiritual imagination – a place of both testing and divine encounter. Here, Jesus faced three fundamental temptations that mirror our own human vulnerabilities: physical appetite (bread), worldly power (kingdoms), and spiritual pride (testing God).

The devil's use of Scripture and Jesus' responses reveal the importance of understanding God's word in context. Each temptation offered a shortcut to fulfilling Jesus' mission, but each would have compromised his fundamental relationship with the Father. The timing is significant – this testing comes immediately after Jesus' baptism and divine affirmation, suggesting that spiritual high points often precede our greatest challenges.

This desert experience prepared Jesus for his public ministry, demonstrating that testing often serves as preparation rather than punishment. His responses, each grounded in Scripture, show that faithfulness comes not through dramatic displays of power but through steady trust in God's word and ways.

Leader's Guide

Group Discussion (15 minutes)

Core Questions:

1. "Which of these temptations seems most relevant to our lives today?"

2. "How does Jesus' way of handling testing guide our own responses?"

3. "What's the difference between being tested and being tempted?"

4. "Where do you see similar temptations to take shortcuts in your spiritual life?"

Closing Integration (8 minutes)

- Preview next week's theme

- Review weekly reflection guide

- Closing prayer about faithful endurance

Leader Notes

Key Teaching Points

1. Testing can be preparation for ministry

2. No shortcuts exist to doing God's will

3. Scripture provides guidance in testing

4. Faithfulness requires patient trust

Pastoral Considerations

- Various experiences with temptation

- Different views of spiritual testing

- Personal struggles with faithfulness
- Questions about God's role in testing

Discussion Management
- Keep focus on preparation aspect
- Balance personal sharing
- Guide toward practical application
- Connect to Lenten journey

Materials Needed
- Bibles
- Writing materials
- Weekly reflection guides
- Desert/wilderness images (optional)

Group Size Considerations
- Small groups: More personal sharing
- Medium groups: Balance teaching/discussion
- Large groups: Structure sharing carefully

Note: This opening session sets the tone for the entire Lenten journey. Help participants connect Jesus' testing with their own spiritual preparation.

Leader's Guide

Week 2 Leader's Guide: When Waiting Means Wonder

(Luke 9:28-36)

Core Session Components (50 minutes)

Opening (7 minutes)

- Welcome and brief prayer

- Check-in question: "When have you experienced a moment of unexpected wonder?"

- Connect to previous week's journey from testing to revelation

Scripture Engagement (12 minutes)

Choose ONE method:

1. **Mountain Voices**

   - Narrator: describes the scene

   - Peter: speaks his response

   - Voice from cloud: delivers divine words

   - Pay attention to shifts between ordinary and extraordinary

2. **Sacred Encounter**

   - Read passage twice

- First reading: Notice physical details (light, cloud, appearance)

  - Second reading: Focus on emotional responses

  - Share what captures attention

Essential Context (8 minutes)

The Transfiguration occurs at a pivotal moment in Jesus' ministry, following Peter's recognition of him as Messiah and Jesus' first prediction of his death. Mountains in Scripture consistently serve as meeting places between heaven and earth – Moses received the law on Sinai, Elijah encountered God on Horeb. Now these two figures appear with Jesus, representing the law and prophets, but they discuss Jesus' approaching "departure" (exodus) in Jerusalem.

Peter's suggestion to build shelters echoes the Feast of Tabernacles, when Jews constructed temporary dwellings to remember God's presence with Israel in the wilderness. His offer, though misguided, shows a natural human desire to capture and contain divine encounters. The voice from the cloud echoes Jesus' baptism but adds a crucial command: "Listen to him!" This becomes especially significant as Jesus continues toward Jerusalem and the cross.

The disciples' silence afterward suggests their struggle to integrate this glimpse of glory with Jesus' predictions of suffering. Their experience teaches us about spiritual alertness – staying awake when we're "weighed down with sleep" might open us to witnessing God's glory in unexpected moments.

Group Discussion (15 minutes)

Core Questions:

1. "What does it mean to stay spiritually alert in everyday life?"

2. "How do you respond when divine encounters don't match your expectations?"

3. "What makes us want to 'build shelters' around spiritual experiences?"

4. "Where do you need to 'listen to him' more carefully in your life?"

Closing Integration (8 minutes)

- Preview next week's theme

- Review weekly reflection guide

- Closing prayer about remaining alert to God's presence

Leader Notes

Key Teaching Points

1. Divine revelation often comes in unexpected moments

2. Spiritual alertness requires effort

3. Glory and suffering interweave in faith

4. Listening precedes understanding

Pastoral Considerations

- Different experiences of God's presence

- Struggles with spiritual drowsiness

- Desire for dramatic encounters

- Questions about divine silence

Discussion Management

- Balance mystical/practical elements
- Welcome various experiences
- Guide toward daily application
- Connect to Lenten journey

Materials Needed

- Bibles
- Writing materials
- Weekly reflection guides
- Mountain images (optional)

Group Size Considerations

- Small groups: Deeper personal sharing
- Medium groups: Mix reflection/discussion
- Large groups: Structured sharing time

Note: *This session bridges Jesus' testing with his approaching passion. Help participants connect mountain-top experiences with valley journeys.*

Leader's Guide

Week 3 Leader's Guide: Finding Grace in Life's Hard Places

(Luke 13:1-9)

Core Session Components (50 minutes)

Opening (7 minutes)

- Welcome and brief prayer

- Check-in question: "When have you experienced unexpected grace in a difficult situation?"

- Link to previous week's theme: From mountain glory to valley challenges

Scripture Engagement (12 minutes)

Choose ONE method:

1. **Two-Part Reading**

   - Verses 1-5: Tragic events

   - Pause for silent reflection

   - Verses 6-9: Fig tree parable

   - Notice contrast between judgment and grace

2. **Dialogue Reading**

   - Narrator: tells of tragedies

- Jesus: speaks wisdom
- Gardener: pleads for patience
- Pay attention to tone shifts

Essential Context (8 minutes)

Pontius Pilate's brutal execution of Galilean pilgrims and the tragic collapse of the Tower of Siloam sparked ancient questions that still resonate: Why do bad things happen? First-century Jews often interpreted tragedy as divine punishment, an assumption Jesus directly challenges. His response moves beyond simple cause-and-effect spirituality to a deeper understanding of grace in life's hard places.

The parable of the fig tree would have resonated with Jesus' audience, who understood the careful cultivation process. Trees typically produced fruit within three years, making the gardener's request for an additional year extraordinary. This image of patient cultivation - digging, fertilizing, hoping - reveals God's persistent grace toward us even when we appear unproductive. The dialogue between the landowner and gardener dramatizes the tension between judgment and mercy.

This passage bridges personal tragedy and spiritual growth, challenging quick judgments while affirming God's patient work in human lives. Jesus shifts the focus from asking "Why did this happen?" to considering "How do we respond with grace?"

Leader's Guide

Group Discussion (15 minutes)

Core Questions:

1. "How do people today try to explain others' suffering?"

2. "What does the gardener's patience reveal about God's nature?"

3. "Where do you see God's patient cultivation in your own life?"

4. "How might this passage change how we respond to tragedy?"

Closing Integration (8 minutes)

- Preview next week's theme

- Review weekly reflection guide

- Closing prayer about finding grace in difficult times

Leader Notes

Key Teaching Points

1. Resist easy explanations for suffering

2. God's presence remains in tragedy

3. Grace precedes growth

4. Patient cultivation over quick judgment

Pastoral Considerations

- Recent personal tragedies

- Questions about suffering

- Experiences of judgment
- Need for hope

Discussion Management
- Balance theological/pastoral needs
- Create safe space for pain
- Guide toward hope
- Connect to Lenten themes

Materials Needed
- Bibles
- Writing materials
- Weekly reflection guides
- Fig tree image (optional)

Group Size Considerations
- Small groups: More personal sharing
- Medium groups: Balance teaching/discussion
- Large groups: Structure sharing carefully

Note: *This session deals with sensitive topics. Help participants move from judgment to grace while honoring real pain and questions.*

Leader's Guide

Week 4 Leader's Guide: The Journey Home

(Luke 15:11-32)

Core Session Components (50 minutes)

Opening (7 minutes)

- Welcome and brief opening prayer

- Check-in question: "When have you experienced a moment of 'coming to yourself' that led to a significant change?"

- Link to previous week's theme of grace

Scripture Engagement (12 minutes)

Choose ONE method:

1. **Character Reading**
   - Assign roles: Narrator, Father, Younger Son, Elder Son
   - Read dramatically
   - Pay attention to emotional tone changes

2. **Progressive Reading**
   - Read story in three parts:
     * Verses 11-19 (The leaving)
     * Verses 20-24 (The return)
     * Verses 25-32 (The reaction)

- Pause after each section for brief reflection

Essential Context (8 minutes)

First-century Jewish audiences would have been shocked by multiple elements in this parable. A son requesting his inheritance while his father lived was tantamount to wishing the father dead, a grave dishonor in Middle Eastern culture. The father's undignified running to meet his son would have been particularly striking, as patriarchs in that society never ran – it was considered beneath their dignity. They would have been equally startled by the father's lavish forgiveness, symbolized by the robe, ring, and sandals – signs of restored sonship rather than merely hired service.

The prodigal's deployment to feed pigs represented the deepest degradation imaginable for a Jewish man, as pigs were considered unclean animals. The pods he longed to eat were likely carob pods, commonly used as animal feed – a detail that would have emphasized his desperate state to local listeners. The elder son's public argument with his father at a celebration would have been another serious breach of cultural protocol, making both sons guilty of dishonoring their father in different ways.

The fatted calf mentioned in the story was typically reserved for major religious festivals or extremely significant occasions, serving perhaps 100 people. This detail suggests the father was celebrating with the entire village – significant because the son's earlier actions would have shamed not just his family but the entire community. The father's extravagant celebration thus served to restore his son not just to the family but to the community as a whole.

Group Discussion (15 minutes)

Core Questions:

1. "Which character in the story do you most relate to right now? Why?"

2. "What does the father's response to both sons reveal about God's character?"

3. "How does this parable challenge our understanding of repentance and reconciliation?"

Closing Integration (8 minutes)

- Preview next week's theme

- Review coming week's reflection guide

- Close with prayer focusing on reconciliation and grace

Leader Notes

Key Teaching Points

1. The radical nature of God's forgiveness

2. The initiative of grace before repentance

3. The challenge of accepting grace for ourselves and others

4. Different ways we can be "lost" while staying home

Pastoral Considerations

- Some members may relate to family estrangement

- Stories of reconciliation and rejection may surface

- Different perspectives on forgiveness may emerge

- Both sons' stories may trigger personal reflections

Discussion Management

- Balance sharing between "prodigal" and "elder brother" experiences

- Guide away from simplistic moral lessons

- Encourage application to both personal and community life

- Create safe space for painful stories

Materials Needed

- Bibles

- Writing materials

- Weekly reflection guides

- Map of first-century Palestine (optional)

Group Size Considerations

- Small groups: More personal sharing

- Medium groups: Mix of sharing and discussion

- Large groups: Use paired conversations for personal application

---

Note: *This parable often evokes strong emotional responses. Be prepared for deep sharing and pastoral care moments.*

Leader's Guide

Week 5 Leader's Guide: The Fragrance of Love

(John 12:1-8)

Core Session Components (50 minutes)

Opening (7 minutes)

- Welcome and brief opening prayer
- Check-in question: "When have you experienced or witnessed an act of extravagant love?"
- Link to previous week's theme of grace and return

Scripture Engagement (12 minutes)

Choose ONE method:

1. **Sensory Reading**
   - Read passage twice slowly
   - First reading: Focus on visual details
   - Second reading: Imagine the fragrance filling the room
   - Share sensory impressions

2. **Character Perspectives**
   - Read from different viewpoints:
     * Mary's perspective
     * Judas's perspective

* Other disciples watching
* Jesus receiving the gift

Essential Context (8 minutes)

The anointing takes place in Bethany, just six days before Passover, making this one of Jesus' last peaceful moments before his passion. The setting is deeply significant – this is the home of Lazarus, whom Jesus had recently raised from death, and his sisters Martha and Mary. The family's gratitude and love for Jesus would have been profound, yet Mary's actions went far beyond conventional expressions of thankfulness.

Pure nard was an expensive perfume imported from northern India, often passed down as a family heirloom or kept as a woman's personal wealth, possibly part of her dowry. The amount Mary used – a full pint – would have been worth nearly a year's wages for a laborer. Breaking open such a flask was an irreversible act; once opened, the perfume had to be used. Mary's unbound hair would have shocked observers, as respectable Jewish women never loosened their hair in public. This intimate act of devotion violated social conventions but revealed a deep spiritual understanding of Jesus' approaching death.

The timing is also crucial – this occurs after Jesus had declared his coming death and resurrection multiple times, but before the triumphal entry into Jerusalem. While others, including his disciples, struggled to accept or understand Jesus' predictions about his death, Mary seems to have grasped what was coming. Her anointing served as both a prophetic act and a preparation for burial, though few present would have understood its full significance.

Leader's Guide

Group Discussion (15 minutes)

Core Questions:

1. "What does Mary's extravagant act reveal about true worship and devotion?"

2. "How does the contrast between Mary and Judas illuminate different responses to Jesus?"

3. "Like Moltmann in the Scottish POW camp, Mary recognized Christ's presence in a critical moment. How do these stories challenge our understanding of grace and response?"

4. "What might 'breaking open our alabaster jar' look like in our lives today?"

Closing Integration (8 minutes)

- Preview next week's theme

- Review coming week's reflection guides

- Closing prayer focused on devotion and sacrifice

Leader Notes

Key Teaching Points

1. Authentic worship often transcends social conventions

2. True devotion can appear wasteful to others

3. Spiritual perception grows through relationship

4. Some acts of love can only be understood in hindsight

Pastoral Considerations

- Different comfort levels with emotional expression

- Various views on appropriate worship
- Questions about sacrificial giving
- Personal struggles with criticism

Discussion Management
- Balance practical/spiritual interpretations
- Handle criticism discussions sensitively
- Encourage personal application
- Create space for diverse expressions of devotion

Materials Needed
- Bibles
- Writing materials
- Weekly reflection guides
- Pictures of alabaster jars (optional)

Group Size Considerations
- Small groups: Deeper personal sharing
- Medium groups: Mix discussion with reflection
- Large groups: Use paired conversations for application

Note: *This passage invites reflection on both practical and spiritual dimensions of devotion. Help participants move beyond simple moral lessons to deeper spiritual insights.*

Leader's Guide

Week 6 Leader's Guide: A Tale of Two Kingdoms

(Luke 19:28-40)

Core Session Components (50 minutes)

Opening (7 minutes)

- Welcome and brief opening prayer
- Check-in question: "When have you seen power displayed in contrasting ways?"
- Link to journey toward Holy Week

Scripture Engagement (12 minutes)

Choose ONE method:

1. **Contrasting Voices**
   - Read passage twice
   - First reading: Focus on crowd's responses
   - Second reading: Focus on Jesus' actions
   - Note the contrasts

2. **Dramatic Reading**
   - Assign roles: Narrator, Disciples, Pharisees, Crowd, Jesus
   - Read with attention to emotional dynamics
   - Experience the building excitement

Essential Context (8 minutes)

As Jerusalem prepared for Passover, two very different processions entered the city. From the west, Pontius Pilate made his customary entry with Roman troops, displaying imperial might with golden eagles atop military standards, armor glinting in the sun, and the rhythmic march of soldiers. This show of force was deliberately timed to coincide with Passover, when Jerusalem's population swelled with pilgrims and the risk of rebellion increased. The fortress Antonia, looming over the Temple complex, housed the Roman garrison that would maintain order during the festival.

From the east, Jesus orchestrated a radically different entry. His choice of a young donkey deliberately fulfilled Zechariah's prophecy about a humble king bringing peace. The contrast was stark – no war horse, no weapons, no soldiers in formation. Instead, the procession included ordinary people spreading cloaks and branches, singing psalms of praise. His followers' shouts of "Blessed is the king who comes in the name of the Lord" carried deep messianic significance, while also challenging Roman claims to power. Their expectations of political liberation, however, would soon be transformed by Jesus' different kind of kingship.

The Pharisees' demand that Jesus silence his disciples reveals the political tension of the moment. They understood that such messianic declarations could bring swift and brutal Roman response. Jesus' reply about stones crying out echoes prophetic traditions about all creation recognizing God's true king, even when people fail to do so.

Group Discussion (15 minutes)

Core Questions:

1. "What do these contrasting processions reveal about different kinds of power?"

2. "How does Jesus redefine kingship through his actions?"

3. "Where do you see similar contrasts between worldly and divine power today?"

4. "What expectations do we bring to Jesus' kingship?"

Closing Integration (8 minutes)

- Preview Holy Week's journey
- Review coming week's reflection guide
- Closing prayer focused on Christ's kingship

Leader Notes

Key Teaching Points

1. The deliberate contrast Jesus creates
2. The political implications of Jesus' actions
3. The transformation of expectations
4. The nature of true kingship

Pastoral Considerations

- Different views of political/spiritual power
- Various experiences with authority
- Contemporary political tensions
- Holy Week emotions

Discussion Management

- Keep focus on spiritual applications

- Avoid partisan political debates
- Guide toward personal response
- Balance historical/contemporary insights

Materials Needed
- Bibles
- Writing materials
- Weekly reflection guides
- Map of Jerusalem (optional)

Group Size Considerations
- Small groups: Deeper exploration of personal response
- Medium groups: Balance historical/personal discussion
- Large groups: Structure sharing carefully

Note: This session bridges into Holy Week. Help participants begin processing the dramatic events to come while staying focused on this moment's significance.

Leader's Guide

Week 7 Leader's Guide: When You Are Looking for Jesus

(Luke 24:1-12)

Core Session Components (50 minutes)

Opening (7 minutes)

- Welcome and brief Easter greeting

- Opening Prayer

- Check-in question: "Where do you most often look for Jesus in your daily life?"

- Link to completion of Lenten journey

Scripture Engagement (12 minutes)

Choose ONE method:

1. **Dawn Reading**

   - Read passage twice

   - First reading: Focus on actions and movement

   - Second reading: Focus on emotions and reactions

   - Note progression from darkness to light

2. **Multiple Perspectives**
   - Divide reading among:
     * Narrator
     * Angels
     * Women
     * Peter
   - Pay attention to each character's journey from confusion to wonder

Essential Context (8 minutes)

The women's pre-dawn journey to the tomb took place against the backdrop of strict Jewish burial customs and Sabbath regulations. They had watched Jesus' hasty burial late Friday afternoon, unable to properly prepare his body before the Sabbath began at sundown. Their early morning visit, carrying spices for traditional burial preparation, represented both devotion and duty. In Jewish practice, proper burial was a sacred obligation, making their mission both practical and deeply spiritual.

The stone they worried about moving would have been substantial – a disk-shaped rock rolled into a sloped groove in front of the tomb entrance. Their concern about moving it shows they expected to find Jesus' body and were focused on practical problems rather than anticipating

resurrection. The presence of "two men in clothes that gleamed like lightning" connects this moment to other divine revelations in Scripture, where angels often appear in dazzling light. Their question - "Why do you look for the living among the dead?" - challenges not just the women's immediate assumptions but our own tendencies to look for Jesus in places of death rather than life.

The initial disbelief of the apostles reflects more than first-century male chauvinism. In Jewish law, women's testimony was not accepted in legal proceedings, yet God chose them as the first witnesses to the resurrection. Peter's race to the tomb and his reaction of wonder rather than immediate faith suggests that resurrection was simply beyond anyone's expectations, despite Jesus' repeated predictions. The presence of the linen cloths without the body challenged any notion of the body being stolen, as grave robbers would have taken everything or left the body wrapped.

Group Discussion (15 minutes)

Core Questions:

1. "What surprises you most about how the resurrection story unfolds?"

2. "The women were looking in the wrong place for Jesus. Where might we be doing the same today?"

3. "How does Peter's response of 'wondering' speak to our own journey of faith?"

4. "What does it mean to look for the living Christ rather than a historical figure?"

Closing Integration (8 minutes)

- Reflect on complete Lenten journey

- Share hopes for continued growth
- Closing prayer celebrating resurrection

Leader Notes

Key Teaching Points
1. The importance of faithfulness even in uncertainty
2. God's pattern of revealing truth through unexpected means
3. The challenge of recognizing the living Christ
4. Moving from historical fact to living faith

Pastoral Considerations
- Different levels of faith and doubt
- Various experiences of loss and hope
- Questions about resurrection
- Desire for tangible proof

Discussion Management
- Balance intellectual and emotional responses
- Welcome honest questions
- Encourage personal applications
- Celebrate journey completion

Materials Needed
- Bibles
- Writing materials

Leader's Guide

- Weekly reflection guides
- Summary of Lenten journey themes

Group Size Considerations

- Small groups: More personal sharing
- Medium groups: Mix reflection and discussion
- Large groups: Structure sharing carefully

Note: *This final session both concludes the Lenten journey and opens new possibilities. Help participants bridge from this study to continued growth.*

Acknowledgements

Hundreds, probably thousands, of people have contributed to this book. There are simply too many people who have contributed to our beliefs and faith to try to mention them here. We carry them with deep gratitude in our hearts.

The two who must be named, of course, are our wives, Debbie Warnock and Sally Stovall, whose love, patience, faith, good humor, and friendship have brought us to this point and without whom we simply could not function.

The Way of Grace

Grace for All: the podcast and the book

The podcast

The Grace for All daily devotional podcast, a five-minute reminder of your faith by believers like you, can be heard each day on Apple podcasts, Spotify, or wherever you get your podcasts. You can also listen on the church website at http://www.1stchurch.org/podcast

The book

In his last days on earth, Jesus commanded his disciples to go into all the world and spread the good news of God's love and grace. It was a commandment that his hearers took seriously.

So does the congregation of First United Methodist Church in Maryville, Tennessee, (where one of the authors of this Lenten study is a member) more than two centuries later.

That's why we began the ***Grace for All*** daily devotional podcast in 2023, and that's why we decided to take the podcast one step farther and publish the first six months of our podcasts in this volume, which is currently available on Amazon.

More than 50 members of the congregation have participated in the writing, recording, and production of these podcasts and of this book. Here you will find a wide range of ideas, a variety of stories and personal testimonies, and an inspiring multiplicity of voices that, in one way or another, boldly carry on the mission that Jesus gave to all of us.

John Wesley, the founder of Methodism, wrote nearly two centuries ago that God's grace is free to all and free for all. We are glad to be able to proclaim that message into our 21st century.

Coming soon: Genesis: The God Who Calls and Keeps

A 12-Week Journey Through the Book of Beginnings

No matter what your religious or spiritual belief – or even if you claim not to have one – the Book of Genesis is a foundational document to the way we live in the world today. It is much more than a series of ancient stories.

Understanding the depth and breadth of the Book of Genesis is vital to a spiritual journey today more than ever.

This 12-week study, presented as part of the Solid Rock Bible Series, will open new and creative ways of understanding this important book that tells us who we are and what relationship we should have to the God that created not only the world but also us.

Genesis: The God Who Calls and Keeps will be available in March 2025.

A sneak preview of the book can be found on the following pages.

If you would like to examine an electronic copy of this book for possible use by your Sunday school or Bible study group, email us at jgstovall@gmail.com. We will let you know when that is available.

Genesis: The God Who Calls and Keeps

A 12-Week Journey Through the Book of Beginnings

Chuck Warnock and Jim Stovall

A Solid Rock Bible Series book

Anticipated publication date: Spring 2025

The book contains four introductory essays to the Book of Genesis and 12 study lessons with ancillary material for instructors and students.

On the following pages, you will find one of the introductory essays and a tentative outline of the lessons in the book.

This book is designed for adult study groups who want to grow in their faith and increase their understanding of scripture. Genesis can be a challenging book. This study offers a deep dive into some of the oldest and most profound of Judeo-Christian literature. While we examine some of the myths and misinterpretations of this book, our emphasis is on understanding how the stories in Genesis are meant to teach us basic lessons about how mankind and God relate to one another.

If you would like to examine an electronic copy of this book for possible use by your Sunday school or Bible study group, email us at jgstovall@gmail.com. We will let you know when that is available.

The Way of Grace

Exploring the Book of Genesis

Part 1: Unveiling the Foundations of Western and Middle Eastern Societies

The Book of Genesis, the opening chapter of the Hebrew Bible and the Christian Old Testament, holds a unique and powerful place in religious, cultural, and historical contexts. Its narratives and themes have not only shaped attitudes, rules, and customs but also our whole view of reality.

How we see the world largely comes from this work that, as far as we can tell, was first written down at least 500 to 600 years before the birth of Christ.

Genesis established the then revolutionary idea of monotheism in a world dominated by polytheism.

Genesis today provides a rich tapestry of creation stories, human nature, covenants, familial relationships, and notably — if you choose to believe in a Supreme Being — a new and intimate relationship between the deity and human beings.

Here are some of the notable themes of Genesis:

1. **Origins and Creation**
   Genesis commences with the account of the creation of the world, powerfully asserting the existence of a single God who is the ultimate source of all creation. In addition to establishing monotheism, Genesis introduces a new quality of the relationship between this deity and human beings. Unlike many polytheistic religions, Genesis portrays the God of creation as intimately involved with humanity, actively engaging with individuals and establishing a personal connection.

2. **Personal Revelation and Guidance**
   Throughout Genesis, the deity reveals Himself to various individuals, establishing a direct line of

communication between the divine and human realms. This personal revelation and guidance create a new relationship dynamic. For example, God directly communicates with Adam and Eve in the Garden of Eden, Noah is instructed to build the ark, and Abraham receives divine promises. In most ancient religious systems, the gods ignore humans or treat them as puppets to be manipulated. The intimate interaction between the deity and human beings sets Genesis apart from other religious texts of its time and fosters a sense of closeness, guidance, and individual responsibility towards the divine.

3. **Moral Accountability and Covenant**
   Genesis places a strong emphasis on moral accountability within the new relationship between God and human beings. The narratives highlight the consequences of human actions and choices in relation to God's moral standards. The story of Adam and Eve's disobedience in the Garden of Eden and Cain's murder of Abel demonstrate the moral responsibility of human beings and the repercussions of their actions. This emphasis on individual moral agency and accountability further distinguishes the relationship established in Genesis from other polytheistic religions.

4. **Covenant and Promise**
   Genesis introduces the concept of **covenant**, solemn agreements between God and individuals or groups. These covenants establish a new framework for the relationship between the deity and human beings. For instance, the covenant with Abraham includes promises of blessings, land, and descendants. These covenants not only affirm the special relationship between God and His chosen ones but also outline the responsibilities and expectations of both parties. The establishment of covenants signals an increased depth and significance

to the relationship, emphasizing mutual commitment and trust.

5. **Development of Faith and Identity**
   The new relationship depicted in Genesis contributes to the development of faith and identity. Individuals such as Abraham, Isaac, Jacob, and Joseph are portrayed as having a personal and transformative encounter with the deity. Their experiences shape their faith, identity, and sense of purpose. This emphasis on personal faith and the divine-human relationship has had a profound impact on the development of religious and cultural traditions, providing a template for understanding the transformative power of encountering the divine.

This overview of Genesis sets the stage for some additional explorations into this rich and powerful piece of literature. The stories of Genesis may or may not be literally true, according to your personal belief system, but they are undoubtedly profound and influential in all our lives.

Genesis: The God Who Calls and Keeps

A 12-Week Journey Through the Book of Beginnings

Among the themes and stories that may be included in this volume are:

Origin and Creation - The Power of God
- **Genesis 1:1–2:3**: The creation story highlights God's power in calling the universe into existence.
- **Genesis 2:4–25**: The detailed creation of humanity emphasizes God's creative power and intimate involvement.

Eden as the Ideal Place (Getting Back to Eden)
- **Genesis 2:8–17**: The description of Eden as the perfect dwelling where humanity lives in harmony with God and creation.
- **Genesis 3:22–24**: Humanity's expulsion from Eden underscores the longing for restoration.

Relationship with God - God's Concern for Humans
- **Genesis 3:8–9**: God seeking Adam and Eve after the Fall ("Where are you?") shows His concern for relationship despite sin.
- **Genesis 4:9–16**: God's dialogue with Cain after Abel's murder reflects His ongoing involvement with humanity.

God's Standard of Morality and Accountability
- **Genesis 3:1–19**: The Fall narrative establishes moral accountability for disobedience.
- **Genesis 6:5–22**: Noah's story contrasts human wickedness with a call to righteousness.

The Way of Grace

The Idea of Covenant - God's Promises to Humans

- **Genesis 9:8–17**: The Noahic covenant introduces the concept of divine promise.
- **Genesis 15**: God's covenant with Abram formalizes His commitment to a chosen people.

Free Will of Humans and the Choice to Obey God

- **Genesis 4:1–8**: Cain's choice to act on jealousy demonstrates the consequences of misusing free will.
- **Genesis 22:1–19**: Abraham's willingness to sacrifice Isaac illustrates obedience to God.

Faith in God's Promises (Patience, Waiting)

- **Genesis 12:1–9**: Abraham's call demonstrates faith in an unseen promise.
- **Genesis 18:1–15**: Sarah's laughter at God's promise and later fulfillment reveals the tension of waiting.

Divine Judgment and Reconciliation

- **Genesis 6:1–9:17**: The Flood serves as divine judgment tempered by reconciliation through the covenant.
- **Genesis 45:1–15**: Joseph reconciles with his brothers, showing divine providence in human conflict.

The Importance of Family and One-on-One Human Relationships (Genealogy)

- **Genesis 5**: Genealogies show the continuity of God's work through generations.
- **Genesis 25:19–34**: The relationship between Jacob and Esau emphasizes familial tensions.

Revelation of God/Mankind Through Story

- **Genesis 28:10–22**: Jacob's vision at Bethel reveals God's promises in a personal story.
- **Genesis 37–50**: Joseph's narrative highlights human frailty and divine providence.

Separating from Others to Follow God (The Call to "Come Out")

- **Genesis 12:1–9**: Abraham is called to leave his homeland to follow God.
- **Genesis 19**: Lot's departure from Sodom exemplifies separating from ungodliness.

God's Surprises and Creativity

- **Genesis 17:15–21**: God's promise of Isaac to Abraham and Sarah highlights His surprising ways.
- **Genesis 29–30**: Jacob's unexpected blessings through Leah and Rachel illustrate divine creativity.

The Frailty of Human Power

- **Genesis 11:1–9**: The Tower of Babel underscores human limitations without God.
- **Genesis 41**: Joseph's rise to power shows God's sovereignty over human plans.

About the authors

Chuck Warnock

Chuck Warnock likes the rhythm of his life. His day begins about sunrise with his wife Debbie and their rescue cat, Buddy. After a hearty bowl of oatmeal, the two of them spend the early morning moments with an inspirational meditation, while Buddy snoozes in a lap of his choice.

Now retired, Chuck previously pastored congregations across the southeast. In addition to speaking engagements at churches, conferences, and conventions over the years, writing became his way to engage with new folks and contribute to the wider faith conversation. He holds a DMin from Fuller Theological Seminary.

Now Chuck has what he has always wanted - more time to write. On his website, **The Rhythm of Grace**, (<https://www.chuckwarnock.com>) he posts inspirational thoughts regularly, and he has several new projects in development. His first book, *The Reconciling Community*, told the story of one church which sought to be an agent of racial reconciliation in its small-town setting.

Chuck appreciates the freedom of his Baptist heritage and also finds meaning in the seasonal rhythm of the Christian Year. He wishes he had said this, but traditionally St. Augustine is credited: *In essentials unity, in non-essentials liberty, in all things charity.*

Jim Stovall

Jim Stovall gets up too early in the morning and starts his day by drinking coffee, tuning in a couple of daily devotional podcasts (*Pray as You Go* and *Grace for All*), listening to Baroque music, and reading as little news as possible.

He spends the rest of his day reading, talking and walking with his wife Sally, writing (blog posts, newsletter items, books, and the like), painting (watercolors) and drawing (pen and ink), riding his tractor, gardening, woodworking, and generally trying to make his day better than the one before both for himself and other people.

In a previous life, Jim was a journalism professor and author of a top-selling textbook **Writing for the Mass Media**. He taught at the University of Alabama, Emory and Henry College, and the University of Tennessee. He spent four years on active duty in the United States Navy. He grew up in Nashville and now lives in East Tennessee.

As a good Methodist, he tries to advance the Kingdom of Heaven on earth by, in John Wesley's words, doing all the good he can, all the times he can, and in all the places he can.

Jim writes a monthly newsletter that can be subscribed to and found his website JPROF.com.

Chuck and Jim

Chuck and Jim first met when they were high school students in Nashville, Tennessee, in the mid-1960s. They shared interests, attitudes, and personalities that complimented each other, and their friendship was established almost immediately. They had no idea that the bond of friendship would be alive and thriving six decades later.

At Maplewood High School, they worked on the school newspaper, joined the forensics and debate club, took many of the same classes, liked the same music, and laughed at the same jokes and comedians of the day. Without realizing or understanding what was happening, they developed not only a friendship but a deep and abiding respect for one another.

The Way of Grace

Since graduating from high school and leaving for college, Chuck and Jim have never lived close enough to one another to visit on a regular basis. The times they and their families were able to get together were the few-and-far-between long trips that each family had to make.

Still, they stayed in touch and never forgot those early bonds. As the years passed, they both came to realize what a rare and special thing their friendship was.

This volume represents a fulfillment of one of the dreams that each has maintained throughout the decades – that one day we would be able to collaborate on an important and meaningful project.

www.ingramcontent.com/pod-product-compliance
Lightning Source LLC
Chambersburg PA
CBHW062110290426
44110CB00023B/2771